MURDER
& CRIME

NORWICH

MURDER & CRIME

NORWICH

MICHAEL CHANDLER

The
History
Press

Dedicated to Ross

First published 2010

The History Press
The Mill, Brimscombe Port
Stroud, Gloucestershire, GL5 2QG
www.thehistorypress.co.uk

ISBN 978 0 7524 5656 0

Typesetting and origination by The History Press
Printed in Great Britain
Manufacturing managed by Jellyfish Print Solutions Ltd

CONTENTS

ACKNOWLEDGEMENTS

My thanks go to: Attleborough Heritage Group; Bridewell Museum; *Eastern Daily Press*; George Plunkett; Louise Betts, Earlham Crematorium; *Norfolk Chronicle*; Norfolk County Council Library and Information Service – to view thousands of images of Norfolk's history, visit www.picturenorfolk.gov.uk; Norfolk Heritage Centre, Norfolk and Norwich Millennium Library; *Norfolk News* and *Norwich Mercury*; Norwich Castle Museum & Art Gallery; and Norwich City Council Bereavement Services.

Special thanks to Gordon Stuart, Helen Byrne, James Broughton, and Mark Holden.

I have spoken to many people and if I have overlooked anybody, then please accept my apologies.

INTRODUCTION

Norwich is a city in Norfolk, East Anglia, which is twinned with Novi Sad in Serbia, Rouen in France and Koblenz in Germany. During the eleventh century it was the second-largest city in England after London. By the fourteenth century the city walls, which extended to two and a half miles, were built. The city was made a County Corporate and became one of the most densely populated and prosperous counties of England.

In 1096 the Bishop of Thetford, Herbert de Losinga, began building Norwich Cathedral. The main building material was limestone which was imported from Caen in Normandy. The bishop moved his Episcopal See (official seat) to the Cathedral Church for the Diocese of Norwich. To this day the Bishop of Norwich signs himself as Norvic. A Royal Charter was received from King Henry II in 1158 and from King Richard the Lionheart in 1194.

In 1567, Flemish and Walloon Protestant weavers came to Norwich and they were known as 'Strangers'. One of this group, Anthony de Solempne, introduced printing to the city. The Strangers also brought with them canaries, which they bred. The canary was to eventually become the emblem of Norwich City Football Club.

Norwich has been involved in various industries in the past. By 1780 the manufacture of Norwich shawls became important to the city and remained in production for over a century until women's fashions changed in the Victorian times. In 1797, thirty-six-year-old Thomas Bignold founded the Norwich Union insurance firm, now called Aviva. By the nineteenth and twentieth century, Norwich had many manufacturing industries, including Start-Rite shoes, Boulton & Paul manufacturing and Laurence Scott engineers.

Caley's was a business that produced chocolate, mineral water and Christmas crackers at a site on Chapelfield. The company was taken over by Mackintosh in the 1930s and in 1969 it merged with Rowntrees, which in turn was bought by Nestlé, who closed down the site in 1996. Caley's does, however, still have a coffee shop in the Guildhall. Jarrolds, established in the 1800s, remains Norwich's only independent department store, while in 1814 Jeremiah Colman produced Colman's Mustard at a water mill at Stoke Holy Cross before moving production to Carrow in 1850.

A fine city – the sign that welcomes you to Norwich.

The Norwich coat of arms.

The Guildhall was the centre of Norwich's government from the early fifteenth century until the arrival of City Hall in 1938. In its time it has been a police station, a court and a prison. Magistrates sat there until 1977 and prisoners were housed there up to 1980. Religious reformer Thomas Bilney spent his last night there in 1531 before being burnt at the stake at Lollards Pit. It still remains the home of the Sheriff's Parlour.

City Hall was officially opened on 29 October 1938 by King George VI and Queen Elizabeth. It was designed by architects Charles Holloway James and Stephen Rowland Pierce. The consultant sculptor was Alfred Hardiman, who helped to design the lions which guard the building.

During the Second World War, Norwich suffered raids on 27/28 and 29/30 April 1942 as part of the Baedeker raids, based on the Baedeker Tourist Guide to Great Britain which was used to select targets of cultural and historic significance.

Norwich is fortunate to have a wealth of museums in the city: the Norwich Castle Museum holds amongst its many collections archaeological finds from all over Norfolk and paintings from the Norwich School of painters; the Bridewell Museum in Bridewell Alley, which is closed for developments and reopens in late 2011, has housed exhibits on the industries of Norwich; Strangers' Hall at Charing Cross is a merchant's house dating back to the fourteenth century, and its exhibits cover the Tudor and Victorian periods; the Royal Norfolk Regimental Museum is situated at the Shirehall and houses the history of the regiment; the City of Norwich Aviation Museum is situated close to Norwich Airport and houses both military and civil aircrafts; the John Jarrold Printing Museum at Whitefriars contains printing equipment ranging from early nineteenth century to the present date; and Dragon Hall in King Street is a medieval merchant's hall dating back to 1430.

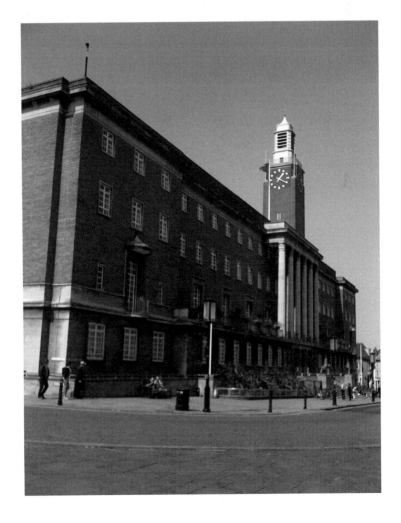

Norwich City Hall.

There are twelve iconic landmarks in Norwich spanning the Norman, Medieval, Georgian, Victorian and Moderns eras. They are: Norwich Castle; Norwich Cathedral; the Great Hospital; the Halls – St Andrew's and Blackfriars; the Guildhall; Dragon Hall; the Assembly House; St James' Mill; St John's Roman Catholic Cathedral; Surrey House; City Hall; and the Forum.

Norwich Castle was built in 1067 on the orders of William the Conqueror (1066-1087). It was used as a gaol from 1220 until 1887, when it was bought by the city to be used as a museum. In 1570 Norwich had one-fifth of the population living on charity, and in 1583 the Norwich Bridewell was opened 'to keep and stay ydle persons to somme honest woorke and labor'. During the period of 1735-1799, 446 death sentences led to 114 executions. These took place at the Castle Hill for the county executions, and Castle Ditches for the City Assizes. The executions were for murder, housebreaking, horse theft, highway robbery, riot, rape, burglary, sheep theft, arson and forgery. Public executions took place at Norwich Castle, the county gaol, from 15 August 1801 until 26 August 1867, and private executions took place from 1 May 1876 until 13 December 1886.

When the Bridewell closed, a new prison was built on the site where St John's Roman Catholic Cathedral now stands. Norwich Prison opened in 1887 on the site of the Britannia Barracks, which was the former home of the Royal Norfolk Regiment. The first execution took place on 12 July 1898, when George Watt was executed for the murder of his wife. Meanwhile, the last executions took place on 19 July 1951 when Dennis Albert Reginald Moore was executed for the murder of his fiancée Eileen Cullen and Alfred George Reynold was executed for the murder of his fiancée Ellen Ludkin.

The following stories are a small collection generated out of a fascination with crimes, both heinous and unusual, committed as part of the dark history of Norwich and its surrounding areas. To keep authenticity I have quoted from court papers and newspapers of the time, using their language style and spellings.

Michael Chandler, 2010

One

NORWICH BLOOD LIBEL

The first Jewish settlers arrived from Rouen in Normandy and settled after the Norman Conquest in 1066. Norwich was one of the first cities in which they took up residence, and the Jewish community later became established in London and York.

At the time Jews acted as moneylenders as it was forbidden by Christians to do so. Money was lent in Norwich to help finance Norwich Cathedral and other buildings. Early history states that most of the Jewish population resided near the Castle Walls.

One Jewish family, led by Jurnet, lived at what is now known as the Music House in King Street and were very important to the Norwich community, which by the twelfth century had a population of over 5,000. Most Jewish people worked as merchants, pawnbrokers and moneylenders, who lent to both the rich and poor in return for pledges of clothes, pots and pans, saddles, gold, hay or animals. The wealthiest of the Jewish communities regularly lent to the Crown.

Thomas of Monmouth, a monk in the Benedictine priory of Norwich wrote a book in Latin called *The Life and Miracles of St William of Norwich* stating that William was born on 2 February 1132. His father, Wenstan, was a farmer and his mother, Elviva, was the daughter of the priest Walward. Her sister, Liviva, was married to the priest Godwin Sturt. William was an apprentice to a skinner and his work bought him into contact with the Jews and they held him in high esteem, even though his uncle, Godwin, warned him against them.

On 20 March 1144 William went to see his mother with a man who introduced himself as the cook for the Archdeacon of Norwich, who said that he wanted to offer William employment at the Archdeacon's kitchen. William's mother was not sure that she should agree to this, but the payment of 3s secured the deal. The next day William and the man visited William's aunt and when they left Liviva asked her daughter to follow them, which she did so to the house of a Jew. William was never seen alive again.

Thomas of Monmouth claimed after the second day of the Passover holiday, William was seized, gagged and had thorns placed over his head. He was bound as though he was on a cross on three uprights of wood and a horizontal bar; his right hand and foot were secured

A glass window of St William of Norwich.

Another impressive glass window of St William of Norwich.

by rope and his left hand and foot with nails. His left side was pierced and boiling hot water was poured over him to help stop the flow of blood. Thomas of Monmouth's main evidence came from a maid at a Jewish house who stated that she saw the crime through a small hole in a door. Other information came from Theobold, a Jew who had recently converted to Christianity and become a monk, that on Good Friday, two Jews took the body to Thorpe Wood. It is claimed that Theobold also told Thomas that the Jews had a tradition that to regain their freedom and to return to the fatherland, they must sacrifice a Christian child each year; a meeting of European Jews was held in Narbonne each year to select a country in which to hold a sacrifice, and that Norwich had been selected.

Other evidence came from a man called Aelward Ded, who on his deathbed in 1149 stated that he had seen two Jews in Thorpe Wood and spoke to them. He claimed that he had not said anything earlier as he had been warned by the Sheriff, John de Canaito, not to divulge what he had seen and that he believed that the Sheriff had been bribed by the Jews.

The body of William was found by a nun and a peasant who informed landowner Henry de Sprowston. Others soon came and the body was recognised as William. The body was buried there on Easter Monday and on the Tuesday William's uncle, Godwin, exhumed the body to identify it before reburying it.

A few days later Godwin stated that the Jews had killed his nephew and summoned them to appear before the Synod. William's mother claimed that she had a dream about being attacked by the Jews in the Market Place. The Jews did not know what to do and their leaders went to the Sheriff, who told them not to attend. He also made contact with the bishop stating that the ecclesiastical courts had no jurisdiction and that the Jews were the property of the king.

Three more demands were made and it was stated that a peremptory sentence, which would mean death, would be passed if they did not appear. The Jews did appear and they were advised by the Sheriff. They denied the charges and they were told to submit to trial by ordeal to prove their innocence. Whilst the trial continued the Jews moved to the castle, where they were protected by de Canaito. During this time, a Jew named Eleazer was killed by Sir Simon de Noyes, who owed him money. The Jews asked for Noyes to be tried, but Bishop Turbe countered the claim by saying that they had to answer for the murder of William before any charges could be made. King Stephen came to Norwich to hear the case, but shortly afterwadrs it was postponed indefinitely. Thomas would later claim that the Jews bribed the king.

Thomas's accounts were second-hand and were not supported by real evidence, as the man who claimed to be the Archdeacon's cook was never sought and the maid who claimed to have witnessed the crime through a door waited a few years before she told her story to Thomas. There is a real possibility that the person claiming to be the Archdeacon's cook was Theobold, and with the help of Thomas of Monmouth he helped to create a story that has caused hatred around the world, right up to the present day.

It was claimed by Thomas that many miracles took place when people visited the grave of William. But was the death a ritual murder? Both Pope Innocent IV in 1247 and Pope Gregory X in 1272 wrote letters refuting that the Jews committed a ritual murder.

Angry mobs killed many Jews in Norwich over the claims that they killed William and this led to the murder of William being called a 'Blood Libel'. It later developed with the edict of expulsion, which was given by King Edward I in 1290, that expelled all Jews from England. It would be 350 years before they returned under the Lord Protector, Oliver Cromwell.

The descriptions of torture and human sacrifice in the anti-Semitic Blood Libels run contrary to many teachings of Judaism. The Ten Commandments in the Torah forbid murder. In addition, the use of blood in cooking is prohibited by the strict kosher dietary laws. Blood from slaughtered animals may not be consumed, and must be drained out of the animal and covered with earth. According to the Book of Leviticus, blood from sacrificed animals may only be placed on the altar of the Beit Hamikdash temple in Jerusalem, which no longer existed at the time of the Christian Blood Libels. Furthermore, consumption of human flesh violates kosher. While animal sacrifice was part of the practice of ancient Judaism, the Old Testament and Jewish teachings portray human sacrifice as one of the evils that separated the pagans of Canaan from the Hebrews. Jews were prohibited from engaging in these rituals and were punished for doing so. In fact, cleanliness for priests prohibited even being in the same room as a human corpse.

Professor Israel Jacob Yuval of the Hebrew University of Jerusalem published an article in 1993 that argues that the Blood Libel myth may have originated in the twelfth century from Christian views of Jewish behaviour during the First Crusade. Many Jews committed suicide and killed their own children rather than be subjected to forced conversions. Professor Yuval investigated Christian reports of these events and found that they were distorted with claims that if Jews could kill their own children they could also kill Christian children. Professor Yuval rejects the Blood Libel story as a Christian fantasy that was impossible due to the precarious nature of the Jewish minority's existence in Christian Europe.

Interestingly, the twentieth century saw references to Blood Libel continue: Hitler used the term Norwich Blood Libel in his so-called Final Solution, while the Catholic Church denounced Blood Libel in the 1960s. Reports of Blood Libel persist to this very day.

Two

KETT'S REBELLION

In 1549 Robert Kett was a respectable, prosperous and secure family man, active in the Church at Wymondham Abbey and a pillar of the Wymondham community in Norfolk. He had everything to gain from land enclosure, investing in property in a period when the land market was buoyant and remained law-abiding. Events that took place at that time transformed Robert Kett into the leader of the biggest uprising in British history.

During the summer months, a group of men went to see Sir John Flowerdew of Wymondham to take down his land enclosures. Sir John was a lawyer and at one time he was an agent of King Henry VIII. Land enclosures had been placed everywhere which stopped the poor from working, which of course put their survival in jeopardy as many starved to death. Sir John bribed the men with the equivalent of 40d to tear down the fences of his enemy Robert Kett. When the men turned up to speak to Kett, he not only agreed with the men but tore down his own fences and decided to become their leader. He made the following speech:

> I am ready to do whatever not only to repress, but to subdue the power of great men, and I hope to bring it to pass ere long as ye repent your painful labour, so shall these the great ones of their pride. Moreover, I promise that the hurt done unto the public weal and the common pasture by the importunate lords thereof shall be righted whatever lands I have enclosed shall again me made common unto ye and all men, my own hand shall first perform it. Never shall I be wanting where your good is concerned. You shall have me if you will, not only as a companion, but as a captain, and in the doing of so great a work before us, not only as a fellow, but for a general standard-bearer and chief. Not only will I be present at your councils but, if you will have it so, henceforth I will preside at them.

Robert brought in his elder brother, William, as his deputy and the men met under an oak tree in Hethersett, which still exists. Robert made the following pledge to a large and excited crowd:

I refuse not to sacrifice my substance, yea my very life itself, so highly do I esteem the cause in which we are engaged.

The men then marched to Norwich, stopping at Eaton Wood, where Robert Kett told the men:

Now are ye overtropped and trodden down by gentlemen, and put out of possibility ever to recover foot. Rivers of riches ran into the coffers of your landlords, while you are pair'd to the quick, and fed upon pease and oats like beasts. You are fleeced by these landlords for their private benefit, and as well kept under by the public burdens of State wherein while the richer sort favour themselves, ye are gnawn to the very bones. You tyrannous masters often implead, arrest, and cast you into prison, so that they may the more terrify and torture you in your minds, and wind our necks more surely under their arms. And then they palliate these pillories with the fair pretence of law and authority! Fine workmen, I warrant you, are this law and authority, who can do their dealings so closely that men can only discover them for your undoing. Harmless counsels are fit for tame tools; for you who have already stirred there is no hope but in adventuring boldly.

Thomas Codd, the Mayor of Norwich, was forced to work with Robert and send twenty-nine demands to the king, leaving Norwich in the hands of his deputy, Augustine Steward. In a short period of time Robert and William Kett were joined by over 16,000 men. The demands were as follows:

1. We pray your Grace that where it is enacted for enclosing, that it be not hurtful to have enclosed saffron grounds for they be greatly chargeable to them, and that from henceforth no man shall enclose any more.

2. We certify your Grace that whereas the Lords of the manors have been charged with certain free rent, the same Lords have sought means to charge the freeholders to pay the same rent, contrary to right.

3. We pray your Grace that no Lord of no manor shall common upon the Commons.

4. We pray that Priests from henceforth shall purchase no land neither free nor Bondy (neither freehold nor copyhold), and the lands that they have in possession may be let to temporal men, as they were in the first year of the reign of King Henry VII (1485).

5. We pray that Redeground and meadow ground may be at such price as they were in the first year of King Henry the VII.

6. We pray that all marshes that are holden of the Kings Majesty by free rent or of any other, may be again at the price that they were in the first year of King Henry the VII.

7. We pray that all Bushels within your realm be of one strice, that is to say, to be in measure 8 gallons.

8. We pray that Priests or Vicars that be not able to preach and set forth the word of God to his parishioners may be thereby put from his benefice, and the parishioners there to choose another or else the patron or Lord of the town.

9. We pray that the payments of castle-ward rent, and blanche ferme (fee in the form of silver), and office lands (kinds of land taxes), which has been accustomed to be gathered of the

Robert Kett in chains at City Hall.

Kett's Oak Hethersett, where Robert Kett gave a speech to the men on their way to Norwich.

17

A view of Norwich from Mousehold Heath.

tenements, whereas we suppose the Lords ought to pay the same to their bailiffs for the rents fathering, and not the tenants.

10. We pray that no man under the degree of a Knight or Esquire keep a down house (keeping Doves), except if it has been of an old ancient custom.

11. We pray that all freeholders and copyholders may take the profits of all commons, and their to common, and the Lords not to common nor take profits of the same.

12. We pray that no Feodorye [an officer of the old Court of Wards] within your shires shall be a councillor to any man in his office making, whereby the King may be truly served, so that a man being of good conscience may be verily chosen to the same office by the commons of the same shire.

13. We pray your Grace to take all liberty of let into your own hands whereby all men may quietly enjoy their commons with all profits.

14. We pray that copyhold land that is reasonable rented may go as it did in the first year of King Henry VII and that at the death of a tenant or of a sale the same lands to be charged with an esey fine [which tenants often paid at the start of their landholding] as a capon or a reasonable sum of money for a remembrance.

15. We pray that no Priest shall be a Chaplain nor no other officer to any man of honour or worship but only to be resident upon their benefices whereby their parishioners may be instructed with the laws of God.

16. We pray that all bond men may be made free for god made all free with his precious blood shedding.

17. We pray that Rivers may be free and common to all men for fishing and passage.

18. We pray that no man shall be put by your Eschetory and Feodrie to find any office unless he holds of your Grace in chief or capite above £10 a year.

19. We pray that the poor mariners or Fisherman may have the whole profits of their fishings as purpres grampes whales or any great fish so it be not prejudicial to your Grace.

20. We pray that every proprietary Parson or Vicar having a benefice of £10 or more by year shall either by themselves or by some other person teach poor men's children of their parish the book called the cathakysme and the primer.

21. We pray that it be not lawful to the Lords of any manor to purchase land freely and to let them out again by copy of court roll to their great advaunchement and to the undoing of your poor subjects.

22. We pray that no proprietary Parson or Vicar in consideration of avoiding trouble and suit between them and their poor parishioners which they daily do proceed and attempt shall from henceforth take for the full contention of all the tithes which now they do receive but 8d. of the noble in the full discharge of all other tithes.

23. We pray that no man under the degree of (Esquire) shall keep any rabbits upon any of their own freehold or copyhold unless he pale them in (confines them) so that it shall not be to the commons nuisance.

24. We pray that no manner of person of what estate degree or condition he be shall from henceforth sell the adwardshyppe of any child but that the same child if he live to his full age shall be at his own chosen concerning his marriage the King's wards only except.

25. We pray that no manor of person having a manor of his own shall be no other Lord's Bailiff but only his own.

26. We pray that no Lord Knight nor Gentleman shall have or take in from any spiritual promotion (Gentlemen shouldn't rent the right to collect church tithes).

27. We pray your Grace to give licence and authority by your gracious commission under your great seal to such commissioners as your poor commons have chosen, or to as many of them as your Majesty and your counsel shall appoint and think meet (suitable), for to redress and reform all such good laws, statutes, proclamations, and all other your proceedings, which hath been hidden by your Justices of your peace, Shreves, Escheatores, and others your officers, from your poor commons, since the first year of the reign of your noble grandfather King Henry the Seventh.

28. We pray that those your officers that have offended your Grace and your commons and so proved by the complaint of your poor commons do give onto these poor men so assembled 4d. every day so long as they (the poor commons) have remained there (at the camp at Mousehold).

29. We pray that no Lord Knight Esquire nor Gentleman do graze nor feed any bullocks or sheep if he may spend forty pounds a year by his lands but only for the provision of his house.

The king, who was directed by the Lord Protector, Edward Seymour, sent William Parr, 1st Marquis of Northampton, along with 1,400 men to end the rebellion. Robert Kett was offered a royal pardon if he gave up the fight. He replied by saying:

Kings and Princes are wont to pardon wicked persons, not innocent and just men. We for one part, have deserved nothing and are guilty to ourselves of no crime, and therefore, we despire such speeches as idle and unprofitable to our business. I trust I have done nothing but what belongs to the duty of a true subject.

The Guildhall, where Robert and William Kett were held prior to their execution.

Norwich Castle, where Robert Kett was hanged in chains.

Kett's men beat the royal army and Norwich was in their hands. Later on, John Dudley, Earl of Warwick, marched to Norwich with 14,000 men. On 26 August, whilst Warwick and his men were having breakfast at the Maids Head Hotel, 1,400 Lansknechts (German mercenaries) arrived in the city with their calvalry, artillery, guns, pikes and swords. The Lansknechts had a fearsome reputation and their arrival was soon heard about on Mousehold Heath and represented a real problem for Kett and his men.

That evening Kett and his men made the decision to leave Mousehold Heath. They had been there for six weeks, were totally exhausted and had lost many of their men. Warwick had made it impossible for any food to get through to the camp and the time had come to fight Warwick's men on open ground. Additionally, a snake leapt out of a rotten tree and landed on the bosom of Mrs Kett; this filled Kett with doubts and many of the men had a belief in an ancient prophecy:

> The country gnoffes, Hob, Dick and Hick,
> With clubs and clouted shoon,
> Shall fill the vale of Dussindale
> With slaughted bodies soon.

In darkness, the men packed up what was left of their camp. They wanted to be one step ahead of Warwick and so they placed their prisoners in front of their army in the hope of a victory.

Another prophecy stated:

> The heedless men within the dale
> Shall there be slain both great and small.

On 27 August Warwick left his footman in the city, and along with his son Ambrose, the Marquis of Northampton, Lord Willoughby, Lord Grey, Lord Bray and others, they marched through St Martin's at Oak Gate. Warwick then sent on Sir Edmund Knyvet and Sir Thomas Palmer to offer Kett's men a final pardon. The men refused this; they had no trust in Warwick as they had seen many of their men hanged in the Market Place, so their loyalty remained with Kett.

Warwick began an attack on the men and shots and arrows were fired on both sides. Kett's Chief Gunner Miles shot the royal standard bearer and his horse in one shot. In the chaos of all the fighting, some of the gentlemen held by Kett managed to escape but the Lansknechts killed several, not knowing who they were. Men on both sides were being killed and people were running for their lives.

As the afternoon approached the fierce battle ended with a large number of casualties. Kett's men had fought for what they believed in against a professional army and paid the heavy price. Warwick had lost some 200 men whilst Kett had lost over 3,000. There were many wounded on both sides and Kett was nowhere to be seen at the end of the battle. The men that were left stated that they would rather die manfully in fight than flee to be slain like sheep.

Warwick then sent a herald to the men telling them to lay down their weapons to escape unpunished. The men answered that they would willingly lay down their weapons if they were persuaded that the promise of impunity would guarantee their safety. In truth, whatever the pretence they knew that this pardon was nothing but a cask full of ropes and halters, and therefore die they would. When Warwick received the men's answer he sent another messenger to ask that if he came in person to offer the pardon, would the men then give up their weapons and accept the pardon? The answer that was returned stated that if that were done, they would believe him and resign themselves to the will and authority of the king.

Warwick went to see a group of the men and employed his herald to read out the royal pardon. On hearing the pardon the men cried out 'God save King Edward' and they were saved. It was at this point William was probably arrested, while Robert, who was mentally exhausted, rode eight miles to Swannington and took refuge in a barn. Some men were working nearby and recognised him and took him to their boss, Mr Riches. Kett made no attempt to escape and was given food and water whilst Mr Riches sent one of his workers to inform Warwick of the capture. The next morning twenty horsemen from Norwich came to arrest him.

Robert and William Kett were sent to the Tower of London and charged with treason. The following is the indictment against Robert Kett, which has its original spelling and is an abriged version:

Middlesex.
Robert, surnamed Kete, late of Wyndham, in the county of Norfolk, tanner, otherwise called Robert Knight, late of Wyndham, in the said county of Norfolk, tanner, not having the fear of God before his eyes, but seduced by diabolical instigation, and not weighing his due allegiance; And also as a felonious and malicious traitor, and public enemy, against our most mighty and serene Lord, Edward VIth, by the grace of God, King of England, France and Ireland, Defender of the Faith, and on earth of the Church of England and Ireland Supreme Head, feloniously, maliciously and traitorously intending and plotting utterly to destroy and annihilate that hearty love and obedience which all true and faithful Subjects of our said Lord the King that now is of this his realm of England, bear and are rightly held to bear towards the same our Lord the King; and to excite sedition, rebellion, and insurrection between the same our Lord the King and his faithful subjects; and to deprive the same our Lord the King of his dignity, honours, and pre-eminences; And in order to perfect and accomplish his said felonious and traitorous intention and wicked purposes, to the peril of our said Lord the King that now is, and the subversion of this his realm of England, according to his power, contrary to his due allegiance, on the 20th day of July, in the 3rd year of the reign of Edward VIth by the grace of God, King of England, France and Ireland, Defender of the Faith, and on earth of the Church of England and Ireland Supreme Head, and continuously after the said 20th day of July for six weeks then ensuing on "Mousholde hethe" in the parish of Thorpe, near Norwich in the County of Norfolk, and at divers other places in the said county of Norfolk, by traitorous proclamations, hue and cry, and the ringing of bells, very many malefactors being adherent and collecting to him to the number of twenty thousand; (He and they) did, as felons, traitors, enemies, and public rebels against our said most dread and excellent Lord the King that now is, Edward VIth, of their unanimous assent and consent, with banners unfurled, swords, shields, clubs, cannon, halberds, lances, bows, arrows, breastplates, coats of mail, caps, helmets, and other arms offensive and defensive, armed and arrayed in warlike manner, traitorously make an

Wymondham Abbey, where William Kett was hanged in chains.

insurrection and levy war against the same our Lord the King that now is. And very much faithful subjects of our said Lord the King that now is, in the same county of Norfolk, did they traitorously despoil of their goods and chattels, the same 20th day of July and during the said six weeks then next ensuing, and by force of arms did they traitorously take and carry them off; And very many faithful subjects of our said Lord the King that now is, who were under the rule and conduct of the most noble John Earl of Warwick, who was appointed Lieutenant of our said Lord the King to subdue, bind and seize the said Robert Kete, and the traitors aforesaid, did they at Dussingesdale in the parishes of Thorpe and Sprowston, in the said county of Norfolk, on the 27th day of August, in the said 3rd year of our said Lord the King that now is, in the said county of Norfolk, with banners unfurled, feloniously and traitorously murder and slay; And the same Robert Kete, and the other said traitors, on the same 27th of August, by the favour of God, were, by the General, the same most noble Earl of Warwick, honourably subdued and conquered: And thereupon the same Robert Kete, as a felonious traitor of our said Lord the King, did from the battle and place aforesaid, the same day and year, feloniously and traitorously betake himself as far as, and towards Cawson, in the said county of Norfolk and was there taken and arrested by the lieges of our said Lord the King, and for his wicked treasons, aforesaid, against his due allegiance and against the peace of our said Lord the King, his crown and dignity: and against the form of the statute in this case lately made and provided.
(Endorsed.) True Bill

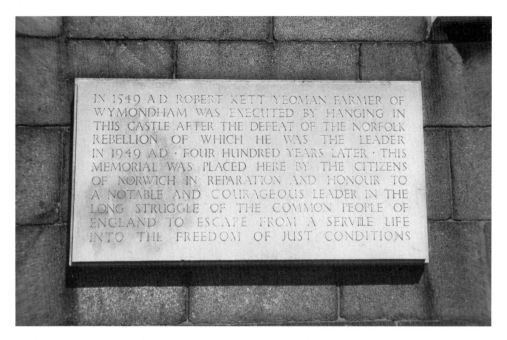

A plaque in memory of Robert Kett at the entrance to Norwich Castle.

Robert and William Kett were both found guilty and sentenced to be hanged, drawn and quartered at the Tower of London. The sentence was later changed that they be hanged in chains in Norwich and both men were taken to be imprisoned in the Guildhall. Robert was hanged at Norwich Castle on 7 December 1549 and his body was then left to rot. William suffered the same fate, being hanged from the west tower at Wymondham Abbey. The rebellion cost the state £28,122 7s 7d.

In 1949, 400 years after the rebellion ended, the City of Norwich erected a plaque in memorial to Robert Kett at the entrance to Norwich Castle, and it reads as follows:

In 1549 AD Robert Kett yeoman farmer of Wymondham was executed by hanging in this castle after the defeat of the Norfolk Rebellion of which he was the leader. In 1949 AD four hundred years later this memorial was placed here by the citizens of Norwich in reparation and honour to a notable and courageous leader in the long struggle of the common people of England to escape from a servile life into the freedom of just conditions.

Three

THE STORYTELLING LANDLORD

John Aggas was a fifty-one-year-old, larger-than-life character who was the landlord of the Lamb Inn, now known as Henry's Bar in Haymarket, Norwich. He entertained children by telling them stories about faries, goblins, pixies and elves. His stories proved so popular that families brought their children from far and wide to hear them.

John had a sister who was married to Timothy Hardy, who was a cruel and aggressive man. On a cold winter's day in November 1787, the Hardys started to walk from their home in Newton Flotman to Norwich. When they were halfway there, Timothy complained to his wife that he had left his knife at home and that they had to go back to get it. Mrs Hardy said that there was no real reason to go back for it, but Timothy said that he would be damned without it and demanded that they return home, but after searching his pockets he found the knife on him and they continued towards Norwich.

When the couple arrived at the Lamb Inn they went downstairs to the kitchen and an argument took place between them. On hearing the noise, John tried to defuse the situation. The Hardys stopped the row and Timothy offered his hand in friendship towards John. As John reached out to shake hands, Timothy pulled out his knife and stabbed John in the stomach, ripping up his belly by 3-4in, which caused a large amount of his bowels to fall out.

There were many witnesses to this barbaric, cold-blooded attack on this defenceless and well-liked man. Very quickly, Timothy tried to stab himself but it was only a superficial wound and he was held by the witnesses until the police and a doctor arrived.

John Aggas died the next morning and Hardy was charged with murder and placed in the castle. At the Summer Assizes he was sentenced to hang and his body sent for dissection.

The ghost of John Aggas is said to remain in the Lamb Inn, reading his stories to all who will listen. The last sighting took place in 1999.

The Lamb Inn, or Henry's Bar as it is today.

Four

THE ATTLEBOROUGH MURDER

Attleborough is a market town and civil parish situated fifteen miles south-west of Norwich. Reports claim that Athla was the founder of the ancient and royal town of Attleborough. In the Domesday Survey, which was compiled in 1086, it is referred to as Attleburc.

Martha Alden was born in a village in Cambridgeshire. She was married to Samuel Alden for fourteen years and she had five children, three of whom died, and the eldest was born previous to her marriage. Martha and Samuel lived in a small cottage near Attleborough. He was known as a quiet and hard-working character, but was he loved by his family? We may never know the answer to this question, but what we can be sure about is that his death came brutally at the hands of his wife, who would later pay the ultimate price for her crime. The couple frequently had very violent disputes and Martha claimed that she was worried that Samuel would kill her.

The good people of Norfolk were first alerted to this case when it fell before jurors at the Norfolk Assizes on 27 July 1807. The charge was that Martha Alden was capitally indicted for the wilful murder of her husband, Samuel Alden, of Attleborough, Norfolk (although it was spelt Attleburgh in the court papers).

The first witness to be called on that summer's day was Edmund Draper. Under oath, Mr Draper said:

I was a friend of the deceased and the prisoner and was with them at the White Horse public house at Attleborough on Saturday 18 July. The prisoner left the pub with her child to go home and with the deceased I carried on drinking and talking to the wife of the publican till nearly 12 midnight. I then walked with the deceased to his house which was near to mine. I was sober and the deceased was sober enough to walk. I stayed at the deceased's house for no longer than three minutes and I noticed that there was a large fire burning on the hearth in the kitchen which was usual for that time of the year. The deceased was in good health and that no ill words passed between the deceased and the prisoner in my presence. I then left for

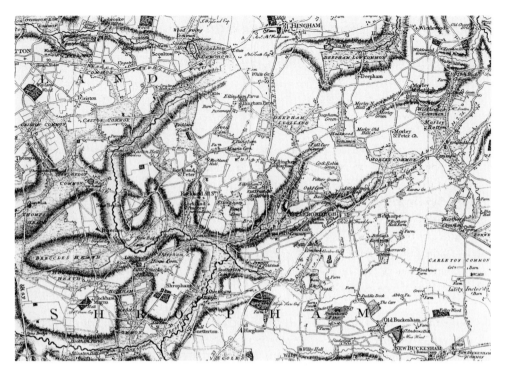

An Attleborough map taken from Faden's map, 1797.

my home in the direction of Thetford. The Alden house consists of a kitchen and bedroom on the same floor and are separated from each other by a small narrow passage. The only other person in the house was a boy aged about seven.

On the night of the murder, Martha met up with two men, Mr Hill and Mr Quadley; for some unknown reason, the latter was not called to give evidence. Charles Hill, of Attleborough, said:

On the morning of Sunday 19, I rose between two and three in the morning to go to Shelf Anger Hall, ten miles away from Attleborough to visit my daughter. I passed the Alden house and saw the door open. It was about three in the morning and the prisoner accosted me stating that she could not think what smart young man it was who was coming down the common, and I replied 'Martha, what the devil are you up to this time of the morning?' She told me that she had been down to the pit in her garden for some water. The garden in question was on the opposite side of the road to the house. The prisoner claimed she had not been long home from the town, where she had been at the White Horse.

You will recall that the witness Edmund Draper stated that Martha had left the public house some time before he and the deceased had left. Mr Hill went on to say, 'I did not enter the house, but I did notice some old clothes lying in a heap next to the hearth.

I inquired about the heap and the prisoner told me that it covered her little boy, who was asleep there.'

Next to give evidence was Sarah Leeder, a widow of Attleborough, who said:

On Monday night, the 20 July, the prisoner came to my house to borrow a spade as a neighbour's sow had broken into her garden and rooted up her potatoes. I gave her a spade which was marked J.H. and she took it away with her. The following evening at about 11 o'clock I went out of my house to the common to look for some ducks that I had missed, and in a pit or pond I saw something floating. I touched it with a stick and the item sunk and then rose again. I did not discover what the item was and left to go back to my home. On Wednesday 22 July, I went back and touched the item with a stick, and to my terror saw two hands of a man appear, with the arms of a shirt stained with blood. I called to a lad to go and acquaint the neighbourhood of the circumstances, and in great shock I returned to my house. I tried to calm myself down after the terrible trauma of finding the body and within 15 minutes I returned to the scene to find the body had been taken out and then I knew the body was that of Samuel Alden.

The body that she saw was horrific and must have made her blood chill, as Samuel Alden's face was cut dreadfully and his head had been nearly chopped off. The body was put in a cart and taken to the house of the deceased.

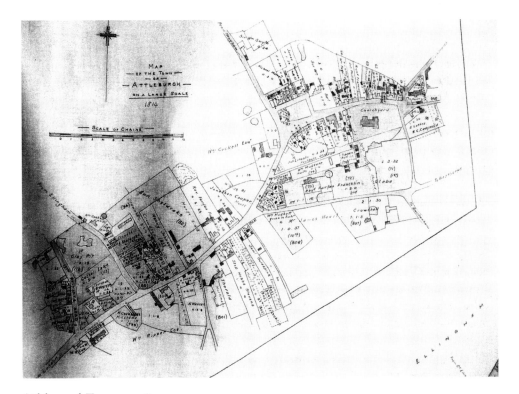

Attleborough Town map, 1814.

Mrs Leeder went on to say, 'I went to look for my spade, and found it standing by the side of a hole, which looked like a grave which surrounded the Alden's garden. The hole was open, not very deep and I saw blood near it.'

The next witness, Edward Rush said, 'On the morning of Wednesday 22 July I searched the home of the prisoner and found a bill hook [agricultural cutting tool] which appeared to have blood on its handle, and also on the blade and it looked as though it had been washed.'

Next to give evidence was William Parson Jnr of Attleborough, who said:

On Sunday 19 July between six and seven in the morning I met the prisoner with a woman named as Mary Orvice, on Turnpike Road near the prisoner's home. The prisoner spoke to me and said that she had lost her husband, and that two men in sailors dress passed by her house at about two o'clock in the morning, and she spoke to them and said that if they overtook a man upon the road, to send him back, but also stated that they gave her an indifferent answer, and passed on. The prisoner was very unhappy about her husband and believed that he was either murdered or drowned. The next day I saw her again and she said to me that she had lost her husband, and that she had been about thirty miles that day looking for him. I was one of the persons who had examined the prisoner's house on Wednesday 22 July and the two following days and stated that the chimney board on the opposite side of the room to the bed was marked with blood stains which bore an attempt having been made to scrape them off with a knife. Blood was also found in a narrow passage leading from the bedroom to the kitchen and on a sack which was found on the floor.

Mary Orvice said:

I known the prisoner for quite some time. I have lived in the house of my father a short distance to the home of the prisoner. On Sunday, 19 July the prisoner asked me to go with her to her house, when there, the prisoner said to me, 'I have killed my husband,' and taking me into the bedroom I was shown the body of Samuel Alden lying on the bed. I saw a hook covered in blood lying on the floor. The prisoner produced a corn sack and at the request of the prisoner I put the body into it and the prisoner then carried the body from the bedroom out of the house and across the road to a ditch by the garden. Mould was thrown over it and it was left. I then left the prisoner. The next night, between nine and ten o'clock I was with the prisoner and I saw her remove the body from where it was last left to the pit on the common. The prisoner shot the body into it out of the sack. The deceased had a shirt on.

The surgeon then stated that the skull of the deceased had been split and there was a dreadful wound on his forehead. His cheek and jawbone were broken and the head was nearly severed from the body.

The prisoner was asked what she had to say in her defence and she told an incoherent story, which seemed to make the testimony of Mary Orvice appear contradictory and suspicious. It also seemed to implicate her in the guilt of the crime, rather than to deny the general charges which had been put to her.

The judge, Sir Nash Grose, summed up the evidence given, and on the subject of Mary Orvice's testimony, stated that it certainly fell under great suspicion, as being that of an accessory to the attempted concealment of the murder. Viewing it in that light, it was to be received with extreme caution. The jury were then directed to retire to reach their verdict.

The jury deliberated for a short while before finding the prisoner guilty. The judge gave a short address to the prisoner and then proceeded to pass upon her the sentence of the law, which was that on Friday she should be drawn on a hurdle to the place of execution, where she was to be hanged by the neck till she was dead. Her body was to be dissected afterwards.

Martha Alden later confessed to the crime. She then gave her own account as to what happened on that Saturday night. She and her husband, whom she said was drunk, argued and he threatened to beat her. Samuel Alden soon after threw himself on the bed, and at that instant she formed the resolution of murdering him. Accordingly, she ran into another room and returned with a bill hook, which she held in both her hands and used to strike him on the forehead, which killed him instantly. She also stated that Mary Orvice had only assisted her at her own request, putting the body of her husband into the sack.

She particularly desired it to be stated that she wished to be rid of her husband, having a regard for another man, but declared that this did not come into consideration at the time the crime was perpetrated.

She revealed that her grandfather had left her husband £50 in his will, which was spent by him at the alehouse, the cause of their first disputes. Martha confessed that she shared her bed with other men than her husband and admitted that the evidence of Mary Orvice was true in substance, but stated that her anxiety and apprehension from the moment of the crime deprived her of any accurate recollection of the facts which followed during the trial.

Martha Alden remained in a very unsettled state of mind during the nights that followed her conviction; and until her execution, she passed the time penitently imploring for mercy. However, at noon on Friday 31 July, Martha Alden was drawn upon a hurdle and executed on the Castle Hill in the presence of a vast amount of spectators – who all removed their hats so that those behind could get a better view.

Five

FRAUDSTER TO MURDERER

The curious tale of John Thurtell first came to light when a story appeared in the *Norfolk Chronicle*, and is hereby printed:

ONE HUNDRED POUNDS REWARD

Whereas at about nine o'clock on the evening of Monday, the 22 of January inst. Mr John Thurtell was attacked in Chapel Field, Norwich, by three men, knocked down, and Robbed of a Pocket Book, containing £1508 in Notes, 13 of which were of the Bank of England, value £100 each, and the name 'John Thurtell' is indorsed on them.

Notice is hereby Given, that whoever will give information which may lead to the apprehension and conviction of the persons concerned in this Robbery, shall be paid the above Reward, on applying to Mr. Thurtell, and any person concerned in the Robbery, who will give information of his accomplices will receive the Reward, and a FREE PARDON. Norwich, Jan. 23, 1821

The reward of £100 was very tempting, but nobody volunteered any information and the following week in the local newspapers it was announced that a commission of bankruptcy was issued against John Thurtell and John Giddens, bombazine (a thin, smooth, worsted fabric) manufacturers, dealers and chapmen. Shortly after the announcement, John Thurtell disappeared from Norwich.

So who was John Thurtell? John, also known as Jack, was the son of Thomas Thurtell and Susanna Browne Thurtell. He was born on 21 December 1794 and had a brother, Tom. His father was a member of Norwich City Council and would later become Mayor of Norwich. The black sheep of the family, at the age of fifteen John received a commission as a lieutenant in the Royal Marines, and he later transferred to HMS *Adamant*. In 1810 he was discharged for unknown misconduct, but the discharge could not have been final because in 1811 he joined HMS *Bellona*. He resigned as a second lieutenant in June 1814, and when he turned twenty-one his father set him up in partnership with John Giddens as manufacturers of bombazine.

Right: John Thurtell, who went from fraudster to murderer.

Below: Chapelfield, where the alleged assault took place.

His father's reputation ensured that people believed John to be a young man who was full of integrity. However, this changed when he went to London to collect a large sum of money for goods sold, which in turn he and John Giddens owed to creditors, and he claimed that on his return to Norwich he was attacked and had the money robbed from him.

We have read the local newspaper report of the incident, and this account is taken from *Jackson's Oxford Journal* of Saturday February 3 1821:

London, Jan 30
On Monday evening Mr. J. Thurtell, of Norwich, was enticed by a fabricated note, just as he arrived from London by the day coach, to call on a Mr. Bolingbroke, near Chapelfield: on his returning, a woman accosted him, whom he did not know, and while walking along with her he was violently struck in the face by some person, and knocked down and robbed of 1508 l. [£100 pound notes] in notes: his pocket, containing the property, was cut open, and a wound was inflicted in the right side, apparently done with a pen-knife. Mr T. was taken so unawares and so severely struck, that he was stunned, and had no power to defend himself. The evening was so extremely dark and foggy, that he could not distinguish the woman's face. Mr. T. had taken the above sum from Messrs. Leaf and Co. of London, to whom he had sold a large

quantity of bombazine goods. It is hoped that as 13 of the 100 1. Bank of England notes are endorsed with Mr. Thurtell's name, the villains will be detected.

Even though he had the wounds of being attacked, his creditors did not believe him and the partnership was unable to obtain further credit and went bankrupt. So what did the future hold for John Thurtell? Later the same year, he set himself up as an appraiser and auctioneer in Hopton. A notice in the *Ipswich Journal* of Saturday, June 23 1821 reported:

John Thurtell
Most respectfully acquaints his friends, and the public, that he has undertaken the business of Appraiser and Auctioneer; and in soliciting their favours, he begs to assure those who may employ him, that he will endeavour to ensure their good opinion by a strict attention to their interests, and also to an immediate settlement of all auctions entrusted to his care. Hopton, June 16, 1821.

His brother, Tom, who was a farmer, was also declared bankrupt due to debts of £4,000 – half of which was owed to his own father. The brother's then moved to London where they set upon defrauding companies. After a spell in a debtor's prison, Tom moved back to Norwich while John got involved with a gambler called William Weare. Soon he had built up a gambling debt to him for £300, which at that time was an absolute fortune.

He firmly believed that Weare had cheated him out of the money. John invited Weare to join him and two friends, Joseph Hunt and William Probart, for a weekend of gambling at Probart's cottage in Radlett, Hertfordshire. As they were drawing close to the cottage, John Thurtell suddenly took out a gun he had hidden and shot William Weare in the face; when he saw that Weare was not dead, he slit his throat. Thurtell, Hunt and Probart then dumped the body in a nearby pond. However, after a few days they moved the body to a different pond, fearing that it was too close to the cottage.

The three men were caught when the police found the weapons on the road. They were able to link the gun to Thurtell as it was one of a pair, and he still had the other one in his possession. Subsequently John Thurtell, Joseph Hunt and William Probart were all charged with murder.

The foreman of the jury was William Lamb, who as Lord Melbourne would later become Prime Minister. The trial at the Hertford Assizes became one of the most sensational cases of the day. All three men were found guilty of murder. However, William Probart avoided the death penalty by turning King's Evidence and leading the police to the body, although he was later hanged at Newgate Prison in 1825 for stealing a horse. Joseph Hunt was also sentenced to death, but this was commuted to transportation to Australia for life, where he later became a police constable.

John Thurtell was hanged on 9 January 1824 and after his death his body was dissected. For 150 years his waxwork was on show at Madame Tussauds. It is said that his skeleton is still at the Royal College of Surgeons in London.

Six

TRANSPORTATION FOR STEALING

Elizabeth Rebecca Furness was born in Norwich in 1804 and may have been born into a Jewish family, although this has never been confirmed. On 30 July 1822, when aged eighteen, she was tried in the Norwich City Assizes for breaking into the house of Elizabeth Daynes during the day and stealing many articles. She was found guilty and sentenced to death.

She was later reprieved and sentenced to transportation to Australia for life. Rebecca was also accused, along with Mary Callow, of stealing cotton, tablecloths and other articles from the home of Robert Murrell. She was found guilty and she left England on 10 June 1823 aboard the *Mary Anne III* and arrived in Sydney Cove on 18 October 1823. She married Daniel Parker from Northamptonshire and they had nine children. Elizabeth died on 17 October 1888 in Kurrajong, New South Wales, Australia.

Seven

MURDER OR SUICIDE?

On the 16 October 1868, rumours spread around Norwich that a woman who lived in Pig Lane, named Ann Frances Clare, had been brutally murdered.

Ann was aged forty-four and was said to have lived happily with her husband, Francis. Francis was employed as a shoemaker and was a former soldier who had served in India, where he sustained sunstroke.

For some time Ann had been confined to her bedroom as she had badly scalded her leg. She ate in her bedroom and her father looked after her, as he lived in the adjoining house next door. He took all his meals with the family, and after going out he left her alone in the house with her husband. At about one o'clock her father returned hoping to find his lunch prepared, but this was not so. He heard noises in the bedroom and presumed that his son-in-law was present. He did not wish to aggravate Francis by calling out why his dinner was not ready as he had a drinking habit and was prone to fits of anger.

Francis was later seen in the yard calling to William Slipper, a young boy working in the carpenter's shop next door, to join him at the Palace Tavern for some porter.

At lunchtime, two girls passed the basement and saw Francis sitting down on the stairs with blood on his hands and trousers. A neighbour, Mrs Shimmons, also saw him and asked him if he had hurt himself. He replied no, but gave no explanation as to the state of his clothing. Just before four o'clock Francis went to the yard and called for William to go upstairs with him. They both went to the bedroom, where Ann was lying on the floor in a pool of blood. William, who was unsure what to do, quickly left the house and spoke with his grandfather and Mrs Shimmons. They all went back to the house, which was now locked, and they saw Francis staring out of the window. A surgeon arrived and was let in and stated that Ann was dead. The police arrived and Francis was taken, along with his bloodstained razor, to the Guildhall where Mr W.J. Utten Browne remanded him until the next day.

The inquest into the death of Ann Frances Clare was opened by the coroner, E.S. Bignold, at the Maid's Head Hotel. He began proceedings by stating that the victim met

Pig Lane, where Ann Frances and Francis Howard Clare lived.

with her death under circumstances of the most deplorable nature. The jury then viewed the body before the witnesses were called to testify.

John Howard, father of the deceased, appeared to be in shock as he gave his evidence. He said:

I am the father of the deceased and lived with her and her husband. I am seventy-seven years old. I have lived about two years and a half with my daughter. Lately my daughter has been confined to her bed with illness. That has been for the last eight weeks. Her husband has always appeared very fond of her and obliging to her. For some time he has been a teetotaller, but he broke out again last Saturday. Since that time he has been much intoxicated. I last saw my daughter alive yesterday morning. She was sitting by the side of the bed dressing to come downstairs. After I had taken her breakfast up to her, I went out to a house near, and returned at dinner time, but my dinner was not ready. I did not see Clare there, nor yet his wife. As there was no dinner prepared I got ready to go out again. I heard someone moving about overhead. I heard a shrieking. It did strike me as being strange there was no dinner ready for me, but Clare being such a curious man I attributed it to his irregularity. I did not go up to ask her about it, because I thought I might put him out of temper. He was not very violent when put out of temper. He never struck me. He had suffered from two sunstrokes he received in the Indies, where he served as a soldier in the 5th Fusiliers. He has complained of his head. My daughter was forty-four. She was right handed. I never knew her to use her left hand. I was back again at about five o'clock. Did not hear anything of the affair until my return.

At this point, John Howard broke down and was unable to continue his testimony. The coroner finished reading out his statement:

My bed chamber is in the next house. The two houses were separate, but I knocked down a partition, and made a communication between the two. I saw him between nine and ten o'clock that morning – having had breakfast with him. He was not sober then. He appeared quite in a deranged state, walking about the yard without shoes or stockings. I always thought him rather light in the head.

The next witness to be called was William Slipper, who said:

I am sixteen years of age, and a carpenter by trade. I have known the deceased some ten months. I worked in the same yard where she lived with her husband. I never heard any quarrelling. About four o'clock or a quarter past yesterday afternoon Mr Clare, who was in the yard dressed in his trousers and waistcoat but no coat, called to me and asked me to go in the house. I did not notice anything particular in his manner, but I saw a good deal of blood on his trousers. I did not notice if he had on his shoes and stockings, or if there was blood on any other part. His shirt was a dark coloured one, and there might have been blood on it without my noticing it. He said 'Come here,' and when I went into the kitchen, he went upstairs, and from the top he called me again, saying 'Come up here, Willie, I want you to help me.' I went up and saw Mrs Clare lying dead on the floor. I did not observe her throat. There was a good deal of blood on the floor, quite a pool. As I was coming downstairs, he said 'Don't leave me.' I however went down and told my grandfather, Charles Slipper, with whom I work, and he went up into the room, but I did not again. The last time I had conversation with Clare [before this episode] was at about ten minutes to one, when he asked me to go and have a drink of porter. I went with him to the Palace Tavern where a young man who works at Mr Blake's and I had a pint between us. Clare was not drinking any but paying for it. Clare was not sober then. I had not seen or heard anything of Mrs Clare that morning. The shop where I work is not many yards from their room, and if there had been any screaming or scuffling we would have heard it. I was there from nine until one and from two until Clare called me.

Police Constable John Smith stated:

I was called yesterday to deceased's house. I went up into the room and found the razor which I now produce; lying on the skirt of deceased's dress, near the right-hand side of the waist. The blade of the razor was forced back as far as possible, and the dress was 'nipped' in between the blade and the handle. I am quite satisfied that it was attached to the dress in that manner, and was not sticking to it by the blood. It was thickly poured with blood, and bore the name F.H. Clare.

Mr Joseph Allen, the surgeon from Tombland who had been called to the scene, said:

I was sent for yesterday to go down to the house. I had not known the deceased previously. I found the deceased lying on the bed, with a considerable gash in her throat. The wound must have been given from left to right. The wound was so serious a one that I don't think it could have been inflicted by herself. I do not think it possible for her to have done it. There were no other marks of recent violence; no scratches or other indications of a recent struggle. The clothes were not torn, but they were disarranged and covered with clotted blood. Her hands were clenched and covered with blood. She was cold and stiff, and I think must have been dead three or four hours. A great part of the blood was dry. This time I saw her was about half-past four. I have not the slightest doubt that the wound, which extended right up to the roots of the tongue, caused death. There was one superficial wound on the left side, and three deep wounds, all meeting on the right. My impression is that the razor swept up, because the wound is slanting into the bend of the neck.

The jury asked if she could have made any noise after the wound was inflicted, to which Mr Allen replied, 'No, because the windpipe was completely severed.'

The inquest was then adjourned until Monday 2 November. Shortly afterwards, Francis Howard Clare was placed in the dock at the Guildhall, charged with killing and slaying, with malice aforethought, Ann Frances Clare. At the end of the hearing, the mayor asked the prisoner whether he would like to say anything in relation to the charge; through his attorney, the prisoner stated that he reserved his defence. He was then placed into custody until the next Assizes.

In March 1869 Frances Howard Clare was put on trial for feloniously and wilfully killing and murdering his wife. Mr Simms Reeve and Mr R. Tillett appeared for the prosecution and Mr Metcalf and Mr Mayd appeared for the prisoner.

The case was opened by Mr Reeve:

This serious responsibility devolved upon myself and Mr Tillett in bringing this matter before you. Bearing in mind the grave nature of the offence for which the prisoner stands charged, that of the wilful and deliberate murder of his wife. For a long period the prisoner was a soldier in India, but he came to Norwich some years ago, and five years since married Ann Frances Howard, with whom he lived until the 16 October. Since the marriage there had been three children, all of whom had died, the third within the last twelve months, and it was said that their death had very much affected the prisoner. Now, the prisoner resided in a cottage in Slipper's Yard, Pig Lane, St. George's Tombland, and the adjoining house, the only other tenement in the yard, was in the occupation of his father-in-law, Mr Howard, who, living alone, had been in the habit of going daily into prisoner's house to get his meals.

Mr Reeve's speech continued to outline the story which had been told at the inquest, before he concluded:

The theory of the prosecution is that the woman was murdered by somebody at about one o'clock – not at ten minutes before one, because the prisoner, who was at that time in the public house, had then no blood upon his clothes, nor was there anything extraordinary in him to attract the attention of those to whom he was talking, but at ten minutes past was he was observed to be so bloodstained that it elicted comment from one of the witnesses. However, nothing more was heard of the matter until shortly after four, when prisoner called young Slipper up into his bedroom and showed him the body of the deceased which was lying upon the floor. You, the jury, will have to decide whether the deceased was killed by anyone, and if you should come to the conclusion that she was, then you will have to determine whether or not the prisoner is the murderer.

Mr John Howard was first to give evidence, followed by William Slipper, and later Police Constable John Smith, and they repeated their statements from the initial inquest.
Ellen Playford, a factory girl, said:

I know Rachael Bradfield, who was at work with me on 16 October. We walked home to dinner by Pigg Lane, in which against the entrance to the yard, we saw prisoner; upon one side of whom dress I saw blood. I saw him go and sit upon some stairs, just at the entrance to the yard.

Amelia Shimmons, a widow residing in Pig Lane, said:

On Friday 16 October, at eleven o'clock in the morning, I saw the prisoner at the entrance to Slipper's Yard, but did not speak to him. At that time there was no blood upon his clothes. Later in the day, when I saw the prisoner sitting upon Miss Dickerson's stairs, just in the gateway of the yard, he said to me, 'Is that you, Shimmons?' I looked at him and said, 'You are in a rare state of blood; have you fallen down or cut yourself?' He made no answer and I went to my house. There was a good deal of blood upon his trousers, and some on the underside of his left arm, left hand, and fingers. I did not stay to observe whether the blood was fresh. The blood was smeared all over his fingers.

Later in the day, about four o'clock, I was sent for to go to the prisoner's house, and when I got there I saw the prisoner and Mr Slipper. The prisoner said, 'I think my wife is dying.' I put my hand upon deceased's face and said, 'Yes, I think she is dead.' I said to Mr Slipper, 'If you take hold of her feet we will put her on the bed,' as I thought it likely that she might have fainted. The prisoner then pushed Slipper out of the way to take hold of deceased himself, and just at the time I took hold of what I thought was a spectacle case, which was lying on the bureau, and I said to the prisoner, 'Here's a spectacle case.' The prisoner took it from me and I have not seen it since. The prisoner then assisted me in lifting the deceased on to the bed. When I instantly observed that her throat had been cut, I said to the prisoner, 'Her throat is cut; surely you did not do it?' He said, 'Is she dead?' and I said 'Yes.' I was going to leave the room when the prisoner said, 'Don't leave me.'

Later in the afternoon I again observed the blood upon his dress. The prisoner also asked me to go for someone as I was about leaving the room. I went out and almost directly returned, when I found that the door was fastened so that I could not get into the house. I called two or three times to the prisoner who was in the house, and who came when he had been called the fourth time, whereupon I said to him, 'Mr Holmes wants you.' The prisoner said, 'I can't come.' I told him that he must come; he came out and I led him to the Tavern. I then said to him, 'Surely you did not do it?' But he made no answer further than saying, 'Give me a glass of ale.' I knew the deceased, who had been suffering from a scaled leg.

When cross-examined, Mrs Shimmons said:

Mrs Clare was lying flat on the floor, but one side of her face was exposed. I did not see the spectacle case until I lifted her up. I saw no razor. There was blood nearly all the way down her dress, and one on her worsted stockings was nearly full. Her hands were bloody, because she was lying upon them. I got no blood upon myself except on my hands, but if I had worn a long-sleeved dress at the time I should have been more stained with blood. The prisoner and his wife seemed to be comfortable living people, but the former was given to drinking, and during the previous week he was very excited, and behaved in a very excited manner, for he walked about the yard without his shoes or stockings. The deceased's head was not too far under the bed that I had to put my arm under it to get hold of it. There was some blood upon the chamber utensil, which stood near where her head was lying. The prisoner looked very wild, so much that when he came downstairs after I called him I had to take hold of him. Though I had seen the prisoner in drink I never saw him look so wild as he did then. When I laid out deceased I saw no mark upon her eye or any wound upon any other part of the body than the throat, except the healed scar on her leg.

Police Constable John Smith then produced a razor case which Mrs Shimmons identified as the spectacle case.

Mr Joseph Allen, the surgeon who had given evidence at the inquest, said:

The prisoner asked me whether it was possible for deceased to have cut her throat herself; and I told him that I believed not. The deceased's hands were clenched, almost closed, which was evidence that she had died with a struggle, but it would be impossible to say whether the hands had clutched anything. We were looking for some instrument with which the wounds might have been inflicted, when a razor was picked up by a policeman, who said, 'Here's the razor.' The prisoner said, 'That's my razor.' I also saw a razor case, like the one produced lying on a chair.

Under cross-examination, Mr Allen said:

The woman's hands and arms were covered with blood up to her elbows. The blood upon the prisoner's person was on his hip, arm and a handkerchief, which he had about his loins, all chiefly on the right side. I also saw the blood was spurted about the room. All the wounds were clean cut.

When asked if one would expect to find irregular wounds if a struggle took place, the reply given was, 'Not necessarily.'

The defence continued, 'Do you mean to say the wounds are not much more frequently irregular when there has been a struggle?'

Mr Allen replied, 'Not if the resistance is great, as the person would then pull against the instrument, so as to make a cleaner cut. One of the wounds was superficial; the other three verged into one.'

The defence then asked, 'Why should there be a difference between the wound inflicted by a suicide and that inflicted by another person?'

Mr Allen replied, 'There is generally a difference in both the direction and the depth. If it had been inflicted by herself, I would have expected the cut to have been in a straight line.'

The defence then asked, 'What was there in this cut to indicate the wound was not inflicted by herself?'

The reply was, 'The direction of the wound in a suicide is from left to right, not obliquely upwards.'

The judge interjected, 'Why should it not go up?'

Mr Allen answered, 'I never saw a case of suicide in which the wound went upwards, as in this case.'

The defence continued, 'Will you pledge your reputation that a person committing suicide would not inflict a wound obliquely upwards?'

Mr Allen replied, 'I will not pledge my reputation that he would not do so, but I will pledge my reputation that a suicide could not cut his throat obliquely upwards through all these parts.'

The defence pressed, 'Is it through being obliquely upwards or the depth that you come to a conclusion about it?'

Mr Allen replied, 'Chiefly the depth. In this case the roots of the tongue were severed so that the woman would have been suffocated and unable to give the turn to the razor.'

The defence then used *The Principles and Practice of Medical Jurisprudence* by A.S. Taylor, which was published in 1865, to show where the weapon had divided all the muscles of the neck, the windpipe, the gullet, had opened the jugular veins and both the carotid arteries, and even grazed the anterior vertebral ligament. Mr Allen replied, 'I believe such a case as that has happened, but it is not stated there whether the trachea was completely cut through. In this case the wound extended through the roots of the tongue; in the other the wound would be lower down in the neck.'

The defence then went on to say:

I should expect a person assailed by another with a razor to protect himself with his hands, which are sometimes out in those cases, though the person might step back; and I should have expected to have found some marks of a death struggle, assuming that the first superficial wound was given by another person, but if the wound was inflicted by someone from behind, the wounded person would not have seized the weapon. I should think that at the time the wounds were inflicted the woman was standing, in as much as there were drops of blood upon the wall, as if it had been spurted there.

When re-examined, Mr Allen said:

The wound, which was nearly the depth of my finger, would require considerable violence to inflict. If a man had stood with his right side near the woman's right side to inflict the wound, I should expect to find blood upon his forearm. The woman, on receiving such a deep wound, would probably fall forward.

Another witness, Police Constable Lingwood, stated during his testimony:

When the prisoner was in my charge at the police station, he said to me, 'I have killed many a man, but I was never so much upset as I was when I went upstairs this morning and found her lying there. An hour after he said to me, 'I feel worse now than as if I had done it.' Ten minutes after, at ten minutes past six, he said, 'It is a silly affair, and yet it is a serious affair.' At about half past six he said, 'I wish this was all over – one way or another. I am sure that nobody else went into the yard, and I was not more than ten yards off. Anybody with half a grain of sense must have seen me. The doctor was the first man we called in. I know it is a hard job, but it cannot be helped. I do not know how I shall get on without her. They are going to a deal of trouble about me, but everyone knows that I loved her too much to do anything of that sort. God bless her! She's gone! And I know I have lost my right arm now. I do keenly and sincerely believe that she must have done it herself, for there was no one else in the yard, and she must have done it between ten and eleven in the morning. I can tell you now I know her murderer, because she told me that if I did not leave off drinking she would make away with herself.

Mr Reeve then began summing up the case for the prosecution, followed by Mr Metcalfe for the defence, each man carefully outlining every part of the case and going over every witness statement to make sure that their points were understood. The prosecution

Pig Lane, as it is known today.

emphasised the fact that it was impossible for Mrs Clare to have committed suicide, with the defence arguing that Mr Clare was innocent. The judge then summed up the case with a lengthy speech.

The jury retired just before six o'clock in the evening and returned just half an hour later. The foreman of the jury said that he wished to ask the witness John Howard whether, on the day in question, the whole house was occupied – the lower as well as the upper room. Mr Howard was recalled and said that the whole house was occupied by the prisoner and his wife, and that they all breakfasted in the kitchen.

The foreman told the court that the jury wished to have the fact distinctly stated because the woman had been suffering from a scalded leg, which might have kept her to her upstairs chamber. The judge said that as the question had been asked, it showed that the jury had paid great attention to the case.

Within a very short time a verdict of not guilty was returned and Francis Howard Clare was free to leave the court; clearly the jury had been convinced that Ann had taken her own life.

Eight

'I MIGHT AS WELL HUNG FOR TWO'

Henry March was fifty-nine years of age and he was employed as a blacksmith for thirty years by seventy-six-year-old Thomas Mays, who was a retired vet and farmer. Mays also employed Henry Bidewell, who was fifty-six and had worked for Mays for forty years. March and Bidewell worked together, but argued constantly and it caused so much anguish to Mays that he suggested the men look to seek employment elsewhere as he wanted to retire.

On Friday 19 October 1877, March and Bidewell were seen drinking together and reports said that they had got on very well. On 20 October both men were at work, with March at Kimberley Hall to look at Lord Kimberley's horses, while Bidewell was at the smithy. By lunchtime, March had returned and struck Bidewell on the back of the head with an iron bar, witnessed by Sarah Bailey. Mays then arrived and asked March what he had done, and as he went to help Bidewell he too was attacked with the iron bar. March then went for a drink before going home. Sergeant John Scott from Norwich met March and arrested him and took him to the Wymondham Bridewell into the hands of Constable Pratt.

On Thursday 1 November 1877, Henry March was brought before Mr Justice Hawkins at the Winter Assizes in Ipswich to answer the charge of wilfully murdering Henry Bidewell and Thomas Mays. Mr S. Reeve and Mr Tuck were instructed to prosecute, while at the request of the court Mr Blofeld conducted the prisoner's defence, as his relatives were too poor to pay for counsel. March was first arraigned for the murder of Thomas Mays and when charged he replied in a clear voice, 'Not guilty.'

Mr Blofeld addressed the jury and said:

I do not challenge the facts of the case, but that there are three courses open to the jury, and the jury will have the chance to consider any mitigating circumstances as to malice, the only

Kimberley Hall, where Henry March was working before the murders took place.

evidence of that was Pearson's evidence. The fact of the prisoner having been in Mr Mays' service so long goes to prove it was a case of a good master and good man. There is nothing to show any malice against either of the deceased men. On the contrary the prisoner regarded his master with feelings of gratitude and he was on friendly terms with his fellow workman. The evidence of the girl Bailey showed that there must have been some quarrel before she first heard the voice in the smithy. The only way to account for the change in March's temper was to look at his own words.

He, according to the evidence of the witness Plunkett, to whom the prisoner first spoke, was first struck at – not hit – by Bidewell. It was true the blow must have missed him, but the fact of its being aimed at him no doubt caused him to go into a state of fury and excitement, in which he lost all control over his actions. So infuriated did he become, that it was a long time before he became calm, and when the Chief Constable of Norfolk, Mr Pigott, visited him in his cell, his appearance was such as to lead him to think he was mad. This being so, could it be said that what the prisoner did was done of malice aforethought?

In his statement to Mr Pigott, the prisoner stated that he first knocked the man down with his fist, and afterwards struck him with the iron bar – the same as that which Bidewell took up to hit him with. What the prisoner said about his master pushing him was not inconsistent with the evidence given in the case. The probability was that some thing of the sort occurred, as the prisoner had said, for the girl Bailey evidently did not see or hear the beginning of the quarrel, and if there was nothing of the sort, how could they account for the frightened and excited state of the prisoner?

I can not ask the jury to disbelieve the girl Bailey, who said there was no struggle between Mr Mays and the prisoner, but what was more probable was that Mr Mays was wishing to stop what was going on, seized the bar of iron, and that the prisoner then in his frenzy thought he was going to use it on him, and consequently attacked his master. Unless there had been some provocation, members of the jury can not account at all for the terrible occurrence into which they were now enquiring. If you can rely so implicitly upon the accuracy of what the girl Bailey had said she saw as to send the prisoner to his doom. No doubt she had spoken the truth, but she must have been frightened and confused, and could she be relied upon implicitly to have stated accurately what did or did not occur? The question for you is whether you can not find sufficient mitigating circumstances to justify in returning a verdict of manslaughter instead of one of murder. Be it one of murder or manslaughter, there could be no doubt the wretched man at the bar had committed an offence for which the most fearful retribution awaits him; but if the facts are such that you should find him guilty of the lesser crime.

The judge then summed up the case, stating:

Whatever might be the result of your verdict, the prisoner has been most ably defended, and I express my thanks to Mr Blofeld, who might rest satisfied that no gentleman could have presented the case for the prisoner more forcibly or ably than he had done. The jury must give their verdict, after considering the case with calmness, regardless of consequences or the pain it might cause you. You are not trying whether the prisoner is guilty of the murder or manslaughter of Bidewell; but whether or not he is guilty of the crime of murdering Mr Mays. This old gentleman's death was caused, I must remind you, not by one blow struck in the heat of anger, but by repeated blows, the effect of what has been described to you by the surgeon. These blows fractured the skull and caused death. And you must start with this fact. These were the blows inflicted. On this point you have the evidence of the girl Bailey, whose manner and demeanour you have seen. She had no ill-feeling against the prisoner, but spoke of him in a way that showed she felt commiseration for him. He saw no appearance on her part of a tendency to exaggerate or diminish the truth; and if she is to be believed, and I see no reason whatsoever why she should not be implicitly trusted, if she had truthfully narrated what passed before her own eyes, it would be for you to say whether in your opinion there was anything to justify in believing that there was provocation which would justify the prisoner in striking these deadly blows.

Malice aforethought does not imply that a man should for a long time have nourished an intention to kill another; but the law says that if a man should kill another, intending to kill him – even if the intention only arose to his mind on the moment – that was a murder. A man was presumed to have intended the natural consequences of his own act, whatever those consequences might be; and no matter how the fatal injury was inflicted, the man was presumed to be guilty of murder, and if there are mitigating circumstances in any case, those mitigating circumstances have never failed to be presented to those who have to advise her Majesty, and to be acted upon in the way of reducing the punishment awarded by the law. It is not necessary to find a motive for the crime, although evidence has been given to suggest of some motive for the prisoner killing his master. The absence of motive is of no consequence whatever, if the act of killing is clearly proved. In this case nothing can be clearer than that it was the prisoner's act which had caused the death of his master. Turning to the statements made by the prisoner, there might be discrepancies of detail; these should not be pressed against the prisoner, but the substance of the prisoner's statements that he had to fight for his own life was certainly inconsistent with the sworn evidence of the girl Bailey, who had stated what she saw passing before her own eyes. But even in his statement made to Plunkett, the prisoner did not suggest that his master had first attacked him, but on his saying, 'Harry, are you killing the man?' he said 'I served him the same.' Although in his second statement he alleged that his master pushed him about, he did not allege that he took up the bar of iron and threatened him, but he admitted that the prisoner took up the same bar and struck his master with it upon the head while he was on the ground.

On to the question of whether the prisoner was drunk at the time he did the dreadful act. In my experience, nine out of every ten of the crimes of violence daily perpetrated were committed under the influence of drink. Drink, however, was no excuse for crime – as is mental aberration caused by the visitation of God – and it would be most lamentable if it were an excuse.

The jury then retired to consider their verdict and came back with one of guilty. The Clerk of Arraigns asked Henry March if he had anything to say as to why the court should not pronounce the sentence of death upon him according to law. The reply was 'I have nothing to say, my lord.' The sentence of death was then duly passed.

It was later rumoured that a Mr S. Linay, from Sadd & Linay Solicitors, Norwich, hoped to obtain signatures to send to the Secretary of State to respite the death sentence on the grounds that the prisoner was suffering from a disorder that at times suddenly cause the aberration of the mind for short periods. This would prove that the killing of Mr Mays was wholly unpremeditated and Bidewell's death was the result of a quarrel, and that the blows which caused his death were struck whilst the prisoner was not accountable for his actions.

On Monday 12 November a letter was received from the Under Secretary of State, Mr R.A. Cross, stating he could not intervene and that the law must take its course. On Wednesday 14 November, the prisoner met with his wife and daughter. As his son was in the Army, he sent his father a letter.

Whilst awaiting his execution, Henry March wrote the following statement:

I had always lived on good terms with my master until last harvest. About that time the potato disease set in, and I assisted my master to take up some that had been planted in a place on which a stack had stood. We came to a place that was very wet, and all the potatoes were rotten. My master got into a great passion. After a time he said, 'We shall not more than finish these today; we will take up those in the field tomorrow,' and asked me if I would help him. I said, 'We are very short of shoes, and I ought to be in the shop to make some.' My master never spoke kindly to me after this. After harvest, in the beginning of October, I could bear it no longer, and meeting my master asked what I had done to offend him, and if I could do anything to make matters right. He said, 'You remember the day we took up the potatoes, and that you refused to help me the next day; it is all over with you Harry, now.' I told him I had said I only wanted to make some shoes as we had none.

Shortly after he told me to look out for another place. He had bought a brickyard with a small smithy upon it, and I heard that a place was marked out for a larger one. Mr Augur, who took my master's veterinary business, went to the brickyard to give a drink to a cow, and he said to the brickmaker, 'The smithy would make a nice shop for Harry,' meaning me, 'if it were a little larger.' Bidewell was told of this, and accused me of trying to get the shop out of his hands, and told me that the smithy was for himself. From that time I had terrible thoughts of murdering him and my old master. I tried to get rid of them and had no thoughts on that morning of doing the deed five minutes before it was done.

On 12 October I paid my rent to Mr Peacock. He offered to fit me up a forge in my garden, but the passage to it was too narrow for a large horse to pass through; but I mentioned it to my master. He said it would not do but if I took it he would stand at my back. I thought he said this only to keep me quiet. On the Thursday before the murder I asked my master, as I was mowing the grass plot, if he would buy a house close to Mr Augur's, if it was to be sold, and make it into a shop for me. He gave me no answer, only grumbled; and I then was certain that he would not do anything for me. On the morning of the murder Bidewell was stooping down sweeping up the shop. He was in my way and I gave him a little push. At this he became very angry and abused me. We quarrelled for a quarter of an hour. He jeered me as he had done before about the loss of my situation, and of his now being above me. The thought came over me, 'Now is the time.' I seized the iron bar and struck him, and when I saw he must die I struck him again two or three times. My master came in, and all my ill-blood being up, I thought I might as well hung for two as for one. I struck him twice. I cannot recollect striking him more. The wounds on his face were made by nails in the wall on which we hang the shoes, which cut him as he fell. Jealousy about the forge and my thinking that I was about to be cast off to get my living as I could, caused me to do the murder. I had not been drinking. I had two horns of beer at Kimberley, and I got a pint of beer on my way home after the murder. The neighbours got me another pint when I got home, but I drunk but little of it.

HENRY MARCH X [his mark]

At six o'clock in the morning on Tuesday 20 November, the Revd J. Landy Brown visited the prisoner in his cell. He also took Holy Communion in the chapel, later that morning. The prisoner was then removed to a room to await the executioner, William Marwood. At half past seven a reporter from the *Norfolk Chronicle*, along with the Revd T.J. Blofeld, Chairman of the Castle Committee; Colonel Fitzroy; Mr H. Robinson, the surgeon; and Mr Under Sheriff Hansell all met at the Shirehall for the signing of relevant documents. At two minutes to eight o'clock, officials entered the room and Mr Marwood pinioned the prisoner. The chaplain took up his position in the courtyard and started to recite prayers while the prisoner walked to the scaffold accompanied by the officials. Once on the platform the prisoner had his legs strapped and he appeared to be praying. Mr Marwood then left the platform, the bolt was drawn and the prisoner fell; death was instantaneous. The body was left to hang for one hour before being taken down.

Nine

THE HAMMER MURDER CASE

Lines on the cruel murder of an old man
Henry Last by name
Good people, give attention,
To this my simple rhyme;
The facts to you I will mention,
About this shocking crime…

(From a song of the time)

On Saturday 14 August 1886, a brutal, cold-blooded murder took place within the City of Norwich. Henry Last, who was a carpenter aged sixty-six, lived in a cottage in Old Post Office Yard, which runs from Bedford Street to Exchange Street. Mr Last owned some property in the area and was known to have kept large amounts of money at his home.

At about quarter to nine that evening, Mr Peter Hoydahl, the proprietor of the Livingstone Hotel who was on friendly terms with Mr Last, was requested at Mr Last's home. The messenger, a young man named Henry Chilvers, explained that Mr Last had not been seen since that morning and that his front door was open and the key was on the outside. They both went to the house. Mr Hoydahl entered the front room. The room was divided into two, with Mr Last's work bench in one part and his living quarters in the other. Mr Hoydahl came upon some clothes and sacks and removed them to find the body of Mr Last. He immediately locked the front door and rushed to the police station, where he informed officers of his find. When the police arrived they found the deceased lying face down with several wounds on his head. The police surgeon, Mr Mills, was brought in to examine the body. As the police checked the house, they found that the key to Mr Last's safe was missing.

Within a few days, various known criminals were taken into custody but were later released without any charges bought against them. The post-mortem showed that a hammer had been used in the murder. One wound laid bare the brain, and was caused

Henry Last's house.

LAST'S HOUSE.

,probably, by two blows from the thick part of the hammer, while the other wounds were caused by the sharper end of the hammer.

The deputy coroner, H.J. Mills, held an inquest on the body at the Waterman's Arms, King Street, with Mr T. Beresford as the foreman of the jury. Mr Hoydahl and Mr Chilvers gave their evidence, followed by Mrs Catherine Redmond. She stated that she lived next door to the deceased, who owned all three cottages in the yard.

Police surgeon Mr Robert James Mills said:

> I was at the home of the deceased at midnight and I found many injuries to the head and I made a careful external examination. I also found a small pool of blood inside the inner room and a little blood was splashed on the inner side of the left hand side of the door.

On the application of the Chief Constable, the inquest was adjourned for one week so that further enquiries could be made. On Thursday a telegram was received by the Chief Constable stating that George Harmer, a plasterer from Norwich, had been arrested by

Detective Mason in London on suspicion of being the murderer and he would be brought back to Norwich to appear before the magistrates on Friday.

On Monday 22 November, George Harmer, aged twenty-six, was indicted for wilfully and with malice aforethought killing and murdering Henry Last on 14 August. Mr Mayd and the Hon. J. de Grey acted for the prosecution and Mr Horace Browne and Mr Haggard led the defence. In answer to the charge, Harmer clearly stated he was not guilty.

The first to give evidence was Mr John Brookbank, a city architect and surveyor, who produced a plan and model of the deceased's house to show the building layout to the jury. Next to give evidence was Mr Hoydahl, followed by Detective Constable Beeston, who said:

In consequence of information received from Mr Hoydahl I went to the residence of the deceased at nine o'clock in the evening of 14 August. The door was locked. When I went in the room it was in darkness. Mrs Chilvers lent me a lamp, and I saw the body lying on the floor covered by two sacks. We afterwards lifted the body up and put it on some planks, and I then saw some blood on the floor near the door of the partition. There was a wound on the back of the head, and I saw blood over the right eye. I examined the house and on going upstairs I found a chest of drawers with all the drawers open and the things in them disturbed. The bed had been turned over and the room was in great disorder. I then went to the police station and sent for a doctor, the body having been placed by me on a plank and tressels.

Mrs Rachael Curl, a resident in one of Mr Last's houses, stated:

I lived in School Lane on 14 August and was a tenant of the deceased. On that day I went to his house for the purpose of paying my rent. That was at one o'clock. The door was ajar, and I went just on to the mat. I asked whether anyone was at home, but I got no answer, and accordingly came away.

Sarah Kemp, a neighbour of Harmer's, was also called to testify:

I live in Wild's Yard, about three doors off the prisoner. On 14 August I saw the prisoner whom I have known about two years. I saw him at a quarter or twenty minutes past seven in the morning go up to his own door. Knowing his wife was not at home I asked him if he would come in and have some breakfast. He said, 'No thank you.' I said, 'You had better come in, you look so bad, and as if you wanted some.' He then came in and had some breakfast. Afterwards he asked me if I would lend him my husband's razor, but I said 'No, I haven't got it at home.' I gave him 3d to go and get shaved. He began to cry, and asked for his wife, and enquired whether she was home from her mother's, who lived at Ashley. I said, 'No, I don't think she is.' He then went into his own house where he found a note from his wife. He brought it to me to read it to him, and I did so. The prisoner then went away to Mrs Savage's, who lived a few doors from him.

Mary Ann Savage, another witness, continued:

I am a married woman and I live at 2 Wild's Yard, two doors from the prisoner's house. On the morning of 14 August he came to my house between eight or nine o'clock. He said 'Do you know where my wife is?' I said 'No.' The prisoner cried and took on very much about his wife. He was in my house a goodish while, but he did not say anything except about his wife. He went away about nine o'clock. I saw him again that day between one and two, when he and another man came past my window. He had a bundle under his arm, tied up in a white handkerchief. The prisoner had also a paper bag with a hat in it. He went to his own house. I saw him again in the afternoon between four and five. He came into my house, and said, 'Do you want to buy anything, as I'm going to sell off.' He was dressed in different clothes. I said 'No' and he said he should sell off and go and find his wife. He went away, fetched a man to buy his things, and afterwards brought a box into my house, saying, 'May I leave it with you?' I said 'Yes,' and he left it and went away. After that he brought a frail basket and asked if he might leave it. I said 'Yes,' and he then went away. The next day he came to my house at two o'clock and had some dinner. He asked me if I would send his box on as soon as he sent me a letter. He said he was going to London. On the Tuesday morning I received a letter from him, which I burnt. It asked me whether I would 'send Mr George Smith's box and tools as he had a good job.' He asked me on the Sunday whether I would direct it to 'Mr George Smith.' He gave me no reason for that. The address given in the letter was 'Mr George Smith, Wandsworth Road Station, to be left till called for.' My husband and I took the box to Thorpe Station on Tuesday night, and addressed it as directed. I had previously put the frail basket into the box.

Cross-examined by Mr Browne, Mrs Savage stated, 'I don't know the name of the man who came with the Prisoner on the second occasion.'

Edmund Nelson, when questioned by Mr Mayd, stated:

I am a sawmaker and live in Lower Westwick Street. I know the prisoner. He came to my house on the morning of 14 August, at about nine to half-past. My wife was at home. I offered him breakfast. I asked him what he was going to do in regard to work. He said, 'I am not going to do any more work till I've found my wife.' I said, 'If you go home and go to your work your wife will come home to you.' He said 'I know my business better than you and I shan't do any work. I have made up my mind to get some money, and mean to go and rob old Last.' I told him not to get such nonsense into his head, but he persisted, and said to me, 'Will you find me a piece of wood.' I told him I hadn't got any. He also asked me for a cedar pencil. I told my wife not to give him either board or pencil. The prisoner stood looking at a wooden partition that parts my workshop off from the bedroom and said 'Let me have a piece off there.' I told him I should do no such thing. He then went into my back yard where he saw my wife's scrubbing board, which he took up and laid down. He then said, 'I'll go and see whether I can't find a piece.' He went away and returned about eleven o'clock with a piece of wood in his hand.

Asked why he wanted the board, the witness replied:

He said he wanted it to go and rob Mr Last with. He then said to me, 'Now then Ted, give me a bit of pencil.' I said I should not, and he then took a file off the bench and marked the board with it. I asked him what he wanted it for and the prisoner replied 'I want to attract the old man's attention.' I persuaded him not to have anything to do with it. He then left my house with the board marked. He had nothing else in his hand, but a hammer before he left and he said, 'I shall hit the old man on the head and daze him.' He then went away. I next saw the prisoner at about three minutes to one, when he came to mine in an excited state. His clothes were disarranged. He was all in a sweat, and looked in a flurry. Drops of sweat were standing on his face. He had not got the piece of board in his hand then. He came into my workshop, and when I saw the state he was in, I said, 'What have you been doing?' He said 'I've just been and done the job, robbing old Last.' I said, 'For God's sake get off my premises.' At the same time he pulled out a white pocket handkerchief and spread it on a box. He next took two revolvers out of his pocket, a powder flask, an old-fashioned shut knife and three rings. He wrapped these up in the handkerchief. The prisoner did not at that time say what he had done to Last.

The witness, who was cross-examined by Mr Browne, denied that he had said before the coroner, 'I told him to make haste off my premises. He said, "I have knocked old Last on the head." He told me before he went to Last's house he would go and daze him with a hammer.'

The judge, Mr Justice Field, read the coroner's deposition, which stated, 'There is no foundation for the suggestion that I had anything to do with the matter myself or was in conspiracy with prisoner.' The judge then added, 'It is quite true that before the coroner there seemed to have been an alteration of the depositions at this point.'

Frederick Todd, a plasterer of 64 Trafalgar Street, New Lakenham, said:

On Saturday 14 August, I was going along Bedford Street between ten and eleven. I had known the prisoner five or six years. He called to me and asked where I was going. He was then about twenty yards from School Lane, and had a piece of wood with him.

James Mace, a cabinet maker from Finch's Yard, St James, said:

I work with a man named Aldred in a room we hire at Charing Cross. On the morning of 14 August the prisoner called at my shop and said to Aldred, 'Please can you set Ted Nelson up with a few 2in-nails and a piece of wood, a foot long, 6in wide. Aldred said he had no time to look after a piece of board.' I went up to the corner where the old pieces lay, and found him out a piece. The wood produced is very much like it. The prisoner said, 'That will be about my handwriting,' and took it away with him.

John Smith, a labourer from Northumberland Street, said:

On 14 August I was near the Bell Hotel, between one and two o'clock with Charles Sidney, John Raby and several others. Harmer came up to us with a white handkerchief under his arm with something in it. He asked me whether I would go home with him, and I said 'Yes.' I went to his house and the prisoner took from the handkerchief the revolver and a double barrel pistol. I saw him with a powder flask, shot flask, and knife and ring. He asked me to pawn the revolver and pistol, and I did so, pawning them with Samuels for 5s. I gave the

The grave of Henry Last, who was buried with his parents at Earlham Cemetery.

money to the prisoner. He gave me the tickets, saying, 'I don't want it. There has been enough disturbances between me and my wife about the pistol and revolver, and I won't have them any more.' When he gave me the pistol and revolver I said, 'What name shall I pawn them on – your own?' He said, 'No; what name you like; John Carter will do.' Old Palace Road is the address given, and the prisoner told me to give it.

After pawning the things I went back to his house with him. He then asked me whether I would pawn two blankets for him. I pawned them with Samuels. The prisoner then went and sold the powder and shot flasks, after which we went to a shop in Rampant Horse Street and bought a hat. We then went to another pawn shop, where he got his clothes out of pawn. Previous to this and when we were at his house he gave me the key which has been produced. Having changed his clothes he said he was going to Thorpe Station to take train to see his wife.

Mr Justice Field told the jury that the key belonged to a Milner's safe.

James Henry Medhurst, a plumber from 31 Stanley Street, Queen's Road, Battersea, said:

On Monday morning, 16 August, I was at work at some houses where I live and saw the prisoner about half past six or seven. He asked if I knew where a man named George Dean, a plasterer, lived. He went away and came back again and offered me a knife and ring, saying he was hard up, and wanted a drink. I bought them for 1s.

George Harmer, the last person to be privately hanged at Norwich Castle.

Benjamin George Mumford, a warder at the castle, said:

The prisoner was discharged on 14 August. [Harmer had been in prison for assaulting his wife.] On the evening of the same day I saw him at Thorpe Station. Harmer said to me 'What ho!' He then told me he was going to Yarmouth, and afterwards that he was going to the Isle of Wight and that his father gave him £10 at the castle gate that morning.

Mrs Rachael Dale of Heath Road, Clapham, said:

On Tuesday 17 August, the prisoner came to my house and applied for lodgings, saying that he had come from Southampton. He told me his name was Harmer. On the following morning he told me he had written to a neighbour to send him his box. I asked him why he did not bring the box with him and he replied, 'I got into a bit of a scrape and had not got the time.' The same day he showed me a letter from Norwich, and I said that I don't think that Norwich was in Southampton. He said, 'No, I am a Norfolk man.' On the Thursday morning he asked me to fetch the box at Wandsworth Road Station. I said that I would do so if he gave me the money. I went to the station and asked for the box, and the clerk coming to the door, nodded to a gentleman, who turned out to be a police constable. After that an inspector came and questioned me. As I was going towards home I saw the prisoner standing in the road. I pointed [him] out to the policeman and the prisoner run away.

Police Constable Hewitt of the Western Division, stationed at Clapham, confirmed what Mrs Dale stated, and went on to say:

I saw the prisoner about 138yds distant from me, standing at the top of Crighton Street. I had a written description of the prisoner, and went towards him in company with the other officer. We got to the top of Westbury Street, which was within 50yds of the prisoner, when he backed down the street. I ran after him. Halfway down that street there is a street called Bramwell Street, leading from Westbury Street to Crighton Street. The prisoner ran down this street and I followed him. He was afterwards captured by Police Constable Bennett. When I got up, the prisoner said to me 'What do you want with me?' I replied 'On a very serious charge.' I then took him to the police station and said, 'You answer to the description of a man who is wanted for murdering an old man of the name of Last at Norwich on Saturday last.' The prisoner said, 'I know nothing about it.' He was detained.

Inspector Mason was recalled, and said:

Since the prisoner has been in gaol I have banged the door of Last's house and found it did not close when so shut, as the lock was not in good condition. There was a Milner's safe in the deceased's house concealed by a lot of boards being placed in front of it. I received the keys produced from the witness Smith. They bore the same numbers as the safe bore. I was able to unlock the safe with the keys. In consequence of information I went to London in the same train as the prisoner's box and arrived at Liverpool Street. From there the box went to Wandsworth Road Station. I went there and communicated with the Metropolitan Police, who relieved me. I received him in custody from the London police, and I said to him, 'Harmer, you know me?' He said, 'Yes,' and I said 'An old man named Henry Last, living in Post Office Tavern Yard was murdered between twelve and one on Saturday last noon, and a man answering your description was seen to go to the house about that time carrying a piece of board. You are suspected and will have to go to Norwich with me on the charge.' I told him anything he might say would be taken down in writing and given in evidence against him. In reply he said, 'I know nothing at all about it. I came here on Sunday by the twenty minutes past two train. I was at Ashby all Saturday. I came out of prison on Saturday morning. I went home when I came out and sold my home off and came up to London.'

At this point, the case for the prosecution reached its end and Mr Mayd summed up the case for the jury. Mr Horace Brown then stood to address the jury for the defence:

It is no doubt that a cruel and relentless murder had been committed, but the question is whether the prisoner is the murderer. Taking the whole weight of evidence it points to no more than this, that someone had committed the murder and robbed the old man, but the evidence at this point stops short.

He emphasised among other facts that there was no blood on the hammer or on the prisoner's clothes. It was also clear that Edmund Nelson had told different stories.

Mr Justice Field summed up the case by telling the jury, 'It is up to you to say whether the Crown has made out their case to reasonable satisfaction.' The Clerk of Arraigns then ordered the jury to consider their verdict.

George Harmer then addressed the court and asked, 'May I speak, sir?'

Mr Justice Field replied, 'No, not now. If you had asked me after the learned counsel had finished I would have let you, but you cannot now.' The jury retired at six o'clock to consider their verdict and returned just five minutes later.

Mr Justice Field addressed the prisoner by saying, 'I have been informed with what you wished to say, but I do not think it would be of advantage to you.' The foreman gave the verdict of guilty and the judge, having the black cap placed on his head, announced the sentence of death. As he was taken from the court, George Harmer shouted out, 'I am not the man. I assure you I leave this dock innocent.'

Whilst awaiting his execution, Harmer made a full and detailed confession. He also disclosed information to the governor which in time led the police to investigate other criminal transactions.

On the morning of the execution, George Harmer rose a few minutes after six, before being seen by the chaplain at half past six, who administered spiritual consolation until seven o'clock. He then had a piece of toast for breakfast and was later rejoined by the chaplain, who remained with him to the last. The acting Under Sheriff and prison surgeon, together with a member of the press, arrived, and the drop was tested in their presence.

At about three minutes to eight, executioner James Berry was introduced to the condemned man's cell, where the process of pinioning was quietly submitted to by Harmer. A procession was formed and headed towards the scaffold. Harmer walked firmly to the drop between two warders, with the chaplain reading the burial service. On reaching the scaffold, the rope was speedily attached to Harmer's neck and the white cap was drawn over his face. With the prayer 'Lord have mercy upon me' on his lips, the drop fell a distance of 4½ft, causing instantaneous death.

George Harmer was the last person to be privately hanged at Norwich Castle in December by executioner James Berry. An interesting aside is that Edmund Nelson, who had previous convictions for various felonies, was promised some remuneration after the case, suggesting that perhaps his statement had been influenced by the police.

Ten

THE WOMAN WITH
TWO SURNAMES

A murder was committed as an act of jealousy on the cold winter's evening of 8 November 1886 in the alley of the Lambs Inn, Haymarket, in the parish of St Peter Mancroft. Matilda Riches, aged thirty, who was separated from her husband Arthur, aged thirty-six, had her throat slashed and was suffocated. Mrs Riches also used the surname Lark and was lodging with a Mrs Howard. As the site of the crime was busy with pedestrians, it would have been virtually impossible for the assailant to have escaped.

On the morning of the 8th, Arthur Riches, a fish hawker residing at Swine's Green, Beccles, came to Norwich with the view of finding his wife to try to sort out the problems that had caused their separation. He came to the Haymarket at about twenty-five past eight in the evening and met his wife near the Star Hotel. He walked up to her, pulled out a knife and stabbed her in the throat. Matilda struggled and tried to grab the blade, leaving a deep wound in the palm of her hand. She tried to break away from her husband and slowly moved from the pavement into the covered way in the Hotel Yard, where her husband continued his horrific attack upon her. Police Constable High was quick to appear and he apprehended Arthur Riches, whilst Matilda was placed into a cab and taken to the Norfolk and Norwich Hospital where she was pronounced dead on arrival. Arthur Riches was taken to the Guildhall Police Station while a group of people with morbid curiosity gathered by the hotel to discuss what had just taken place.

At the court in the Guildhall on the day after the murder, Arthur Riches was placed in the dock, undefended, before Magistrate F.W. Harmer, Under Magistrate R. Fitch, Sheriff W.J. Utten Browne, Under Sheriff J.D. Smith, Prosecutor T. Wells and Under Prosecutor S. Newton. The Town Clerk, who was leading the prosecution, opened up the case by stating that the deceased had left her husband two weeks ago and stayed at a public house in Norwich before moving in with Mrs Amelia Howard at 64 Colegate Street. On the

Haymarket, near the Star Hotel where the murder of Matilda Riches took place.

night of the murder, the prisoner was accompanied to Norwich by his father, who was worried about his behaviour. After attacking his wife he gave the knife to his father before the police took it, but Mr Riches Snr promptly gave it to the police as soon as he could.

The first witness called was Amelia Howard, who said:

> Last evening at about a quarter past eight I was walking by the Star Hotel, Haymarket, with the deceased, who was known to me as Matilda Lark, we had then come from the Victoria Station. She had been lodging with me since last Friday week, 29 October. She was staying with me up to last Monday. We met two men, one of whom was the prisoner. The other one was an old man. I did not know either of them at the time, but I have since heard that the elder was the prisoner's father. The prisoner spoke to Mrs Lark saying, 'What have you been doing here?' she replied, 'I shan't tell you.' The prisoner then said 'Where are you going?' she answered, 'I am going home with Mrs Howard, this is my landlady.' I said 'Who are you to insult this friend of mine?' The deceased said 'This is my husband.' The prisoner then made a pull at one of her earrings and said 'Where did you get these?' I said, 'Don't break them, they are mine, I lent them to her for today.' I caught the ear drop as it fell from her ear. I don't think he said any more but he knocked deceased's head against the doorway of the shop next to the hotel.

Mr Riches Snr, who was in the courtroom, then interrupted to say that Mrs Howard was going too far, prompting the chairman to warn him to behave himself. Mrs Howard continued but a further outburst took place and Mr Riches Snr was removed from the court. Mrs Howard continued by saying:

He knocked her head two or three times against the shop door. The deceased called out 'Oh, Mrs Howard, he's got a knife.' I saw something shine like a knife, and I observed blood running down from her face on to her arm. Some blood went on to me. I said to the prisoner, 'Oh, pray don't. Let her explain herself.' The prisoner's left arm seemed to be round the back of her neck. That was just before I saw the blood flowing from her face. The deceased called out 'Oh!' and staggered round the corner into the Star Yard. At the same time the prisoner's father was clinging to him. He got hold of his arm and tried to pull him back. The prisoner seemed stronger than his father, and pulled him into the yard with him. I saw the prisoner's right hand move in front of his wife's throat two or three times. The prisoner said, 'I'll be hung for you.' I then shouted for the police. When I turned round again I saw her drop down against the wall. She made a slight groaning noise. The prisoner was very close to her, and I believe he had hold of her hand. I called her 'Tilly' and I heard her make a noise with her throat.

A policeman came up and I and the deceased woman were put into a cab and taken to the hospital. Some man also got into the cab, put a handkerchief round her throat, and tried to stop the bleeding. During the time we were in the cab she did not speak or groan, but I heard a slight noise in her throat when we got as far as Stocking's, the butcher shop, in St Stephen's, which is about halfway from the Star to the hospital.

Mrs Howard was then cross-examined by the prisoner but was reprimanded on one occasion by the clerk over his remarks.

John Riches, the father of the prisoner, was then led back into the courtroom in order to testify:

Last evening about eight o'clock I met my son from the Star Hotel. I told to him I did not expect to see him there and that he had better have kept at Beccles. I said, 'I shouldn't have troubled after her,' meaning his wife. I knew at the time that his wife had left him. After that I walked with him a little way and we met his wife with the last witness, Mrs Howard. He stopped his wife and spoke, asking here where she was going. She said "I am going my way and you can do the same.' He next asked her where she was lodging, and she replied, 'At respectable lodgings.' The prisoner said to her, 'What have you got in your ears?' meaning the eardrops, and the last witness replied, 'They are mine.' After that he said 'Whose brooch is this you are wearing?' It seemed to me as if he was going to pull it off, but I don't know whether she made an answer. She affronted him by saying, 'I have heard an account of how you have been going on.' She meant that he had been about with other women.

Mr Browne from the bench asked if she made use of these words, and Mr Riches replied:

No, but that is what she meant. I can defy anyone to write to Mr Barber of Beccles to get his character. After he had plucked her earrings out and went at the brooch in her breast, I thought he had got a knife. I seized hold of his right arm and tried to stop him all I could. I followed him and his wife down the Star Yard, and tried to do what I could to keep him from her. I can't say whether he went up to her in the Star Yard. I was looking too much after him to see what he did. I saw some blood. I can't say whether it came from her throat or whether it came from her at all. I had some on my hands. I did not see any blood till he and I went up to her. I did not see any before, and it's no use saying I did. I saw a man standing with a handkerchief up to her face. At the time prisoner gave me the knife and he said, 'I'll give you this knife.'

The Town Clerk then asked, 'Did he say when he gave you the knife, "I'll be hung for her?"' Mr Riches replied that he could not recollect this.

William Denny Balls, a bystander who witnessed the incident, said:

Last evening at about eight I saw a man and woman struggling in a doorway adjourning the Star Hotel. I know the prisoner to be the man. The prisoner pushed the woman into the doorway, put his arm across her shoulder and around her neck. I heard him say at that moment, 'I'll kill you and be hung for it.' His father got hold of him and the woman got away from the prisoner and went down the Star Yard. The prisoner struggled to get from his father, released himself, and went down the yard after her. He overtook the woman, put his left arm round her neck, and struck her two or three blows. I thought it was with his fist, for I did not see a knife. She fell down against the sole door of the bar in the entrance to the yard, and I saw a wound on the side of her neck. The prisoner caught hold of her hand and kept shaking it, saying, 'Goodbye Matilda, I shan't see you any more.'

A further witness, Arthur Pegg, said:

Last evening I was near the Star Hotel at about ten minutes or a quarter past eight, and saw two men struggling. The elder one was trying to keep the other back, and I thought it was a quarrel between them. I saw the younger get away from the elder one, and saw something bright in his hand. I heard some one call out 'He's got a knife.' The man ran into the entrance to the yard and I followed him. I then saw him with his left arm round a woman's neck, and it seemed as if he was striking her on the left side. I next saw a young man supporting the woman, who was bleeding, and afterwards saw the prisoner and another man at the bottom of the yard.

Police Constable High testified:

Last evening at a quarter past eight, I was called to the Star Hotel, Haymarket. I saw a woman there supported by two men. She was bleeding from wounds on the face and also from the neck. I asked generally who had done it and the prisoner replied, 'I did.' Turning to the woman he said 'I'll be hung for you.' I told the prisoner I should take him into custody on a charge of stabbing the woman. The prisoner said 'Stop a moment.' He then shook hands with his wife and bade her goodbye. I then took him to the police station.

Police Sergeant Meal said:

Orford Place, Lamb Inn Yard, near the Star Hotel.

Number 64 Colegate, the home of Mrs Howard where Matilda Riches (Lark) lodged.

I was in charge at the police station at quarter past eight on Monday evening. The prisoner was brought in at twenty past eight on a charge of stabbing a woman. He said 'If she dies I'll die too. I did it in the street. I hope she will die. I gave the knife to my father.' When told about twenty minutes afterwards that his wife was dead, he said, 'Then I'll die too.'

Mr R.J. Mills, a surgeon for the police force, stated, 'Last evening I went to the police station and saw the prisoner. His hands were covered in blood.'

The bench then committed Arthur Riches for trial at the Assizes. At the trial he was indicted for feloniously, wilfully, and of malice aforethought killing and murdering Matilda Riches on 8 November. The prisoner pleaded not guilty. Mr Mayd and Mr Malden led the prosecution and Mr J.P. Grain acted for the defence. Mr Mayd opened up the case by stating that the couple had been married for two years, but their marriage had not been a happy one. On 29 October Mrs Riches left her husband and came to Norwich, where she resided with Mrs Howard and used the surname Lark. A post-mortem examination revealed the fact that the deceased died not from the cut in the throat but from strangulation, a bone in the throat having been broken. Mr Mayd also told the court that he would be calling a woman named Donnington, who on 8 October heard the prisoner threaten his wife at Beccles, and also a man named Farman, who saw the prisoner when he arrived at Norwich, where he said that he had been to look for his wife and that he was willing to forgive her for the past if she came home. He also added that he would kill her and a man named Lark if he caught them together, upon which he took out a knife and sharpened it on a stone.

Mr Grain began the defence by saying:

> This was a most painful case. It was a most pathetic story that was told in the few words of the gatekeeper at Beccles [whom Riches had seen on the morning of the murder] of what the prisoner said to him in his excited state. The prisoner said that, 'We would have lived happily if this man had not come across us.'

Mr Grain then went on to say, 'The prisoner was being tried for committing this act of malice aforethought. But there was another alternative. If the jury thought that prisoner, though he caused the woman's death, had no malice aforethought, then he was not guilty of murder, but of manslaughter.'

The judge interrupted by saying, 'What evidence is there to reduce the crime to manslaughter? For my sake will you point out to me what evidence there is that can possibly reduce this crime to manslaughter?'

Mr Grain replied:

> There was a state of circumstances that the jury might find a verdict of manslaughter. When the prisoner had pulled out one earring he took out his knife, not for the purpose of cutting the woman's throat, but for purpose of cutting off the earring. She being a powerful woman undoubtedly resisted. The prisoner, however, held her tightly. Suppose that in the attempt to take his wife's earring only he had inflicted the wound which had been described near the ear. That wound was a superficial one. Assuming that it was possible that the injury was inflicted without any intention on the part of the prisoner to take the life of his wife, even despite the threats of 8 October and 26 October, considering the serious nature of the crime which was charged against prisoner, and that the jury should look at the evidence narrowly.

The judge interrupted and said 'I will ask the jury to look at the evidence dispassionately, and not narrowly. I will inform the jury what the law is, and they must look at the evidence in a similar way as if the charge related to stealing a pocket handkerchief.'

In continuing, Mr Grain said:

> I suggest that there is a reasonable possibility that his proposition was true, that the man had no intention at the moment of killing his wife, and that what he said about 'hung for his wife,' and 'swinging for her' was only mere ignorant words. What the prisoner said upon being told that his wife was dead, 'I shall be hung for her,' was capable of being interpreted in another way than that suggested.

Once again the judge interrupted to say the act of killing was not *prima facie* evidence of an intention of murder, and he should deal with the law upon that point.

Mr Grain replied:

That it was so, but I state that in this case there was no intention to kill, but that prisoner had simply come to Norwich to induce his wife to return home. However much the man might repent at the next moment, that was no answer in law. But did the prisoner, when he took hold of his wife, intend to kill and slay her? I suggest that it was an unlawful act done in anger, solely for the purpose of cutting away the things in the ear. Directly the prisoner saw the woman on the ground he asked her to shake hands. She was not able. I would have hoped that she would have done so if she could. This showed that there was no malice, no intention to kill, and that the unlawful act committed was one of manslaughter. On behalf of the prisoner I besought to jury to accept the proposition that I have put before them.

In his summing up, the judge said that the jury must do their duty in this as in other cases. He made clear that they must let nothing induce them to swerve from the due administration of the law and it would be a bad day for this country if juries were led by sympathy.

The jury retired at three minutes to one in the afternoon and returned just eighteen minutes later. The Clerk of Arraigns asked, 'Are you agreed upon your verdict?'

The foreman of the jury replied, 'Yes.'

The clerk continued, 'Do you find the prisoner at the bar guilty or not guilty?'

The foreman began to reply, 'My Lord —' before the judge interjected: 'Do not make any statement, but answer the question to you.'

The clerk repeated, 'Do you find the prisoner guilty of murder?'

The foreman answered, 'We find him guilty of murder, but with a strong recommendation to mercy on account of great provocation.'

The Clerk of Arraigns then addressed the prisoner: 'Arthur Riches, you stand convicted of the crime of wilful murder. What have you to say why the court should not give you judgement according to law?'

Arthur Riches made no reply. The judge then made this speech, which is reproduced in full:

There could be no alternative for the jury. It is not my habit when it is my duty to pass sentence in a case of this kind to make any observation upon it, or in any way to increase the pain and distress under which you may at the present moment be labouring, but I think it in this case right to say that it ought to be well and widely understood throughout the length and breadth of the land, and by everybody concerned in life, or in administering the affairs of life, that whatever may have been the conduct of your wife there is no justification whatever for the acts of which you have been found guilty. There is no justification in law, because the law does not permit the sanctity of human life to be invaded for any cause of jealousy between man and wife or for the love of one person for another. Nothing of that kind is sanctioned by the law of this country. I know enough, I will not only say of the laws of other countries, but of the habits of tribunals in other countries to know that in many cases like this the justice of the land is tampered with for the sake of their supposed model constitutions. But I am glad to find that in this country the juries uphold the law of the land, and follow the direction laid down by the law in finding a conscientious verdict. I thank them for that.

No one who has heard the trial can doubt that it is possible that you have been badly treated, but do not let anybody who has heard this trial or anybody who has read what has taken place imagine that such conduct if it were the worst in the world, is any justifications for the cruel murder in which you destroyed that poor woman's life. The jury, having conscientiously done their duty, have accompanied their verdict with a strong recommendation to mercy, and it will be my duty to take care that the recommendation is laid before the Queen, who is the fountain of mercy in this kingdom, but meanwhile I have but one duty to perform, and is to pass upon you the sentence which the law dictates in a case of this kind, and it is that you be taken from hence to the place whence you came, and from there to a place of execution, that you be there hanged by the neck until you shall be dead, and that your body be afterwards buried within the precincts of the prison in which you shall last have been confined after your conviction. And may the Lord have mercy upon your soul.

Arthur Riches touched his forehead and thanked the judge.

The sentence was later commuted to a life sentence in prison and he died whilst in HMP Parkhurst in 1898.

Eleven

THE NORWICH INVINCIBLE

In 1883 Joseph Betts was charged with writing numerous threatening letters to the Lord Bishop of Norwich and Mr Colman MP under the disguise of 'The Norwich Invincible', stating that he had been appointed an agent of a secret society, the objective of which was to put to death certain persons who were unwilling to conform with its demands. He was found guilty and sent to prison. From that point onwards, he laboured an idea of some real or imaginary grievance to the police in general, especially Police Constable James Southgate of the Norwich Police Force.

On Thursday 21 February 1889 at Northumberland Street off Dereham Road, Joseph Betts made an attempt to murder Police Constable James Southgate by firing his revolver at him. At eleven o'clock Mr R. Hitchman, the Chief Constable, applied to the magistrates at the police court for a warrant for the apprehension of the perpetrator. The magistrates read the report, which stated that at just after half past six that morning Police Constable Southgate was on his way home from night duty to his home in Northumberland Street. When he passed a row of houses known as Victoria Terrace at the Dereham Road end, he was met by Betts, who lived in the second house in the terrace. Betts said something to Police Constable Southgate, and when asked what he meant, Betts said that he did not intend to have any more false charges brought against him by the police.

Betts took from his pocket a six-chambered revolver and aimed it at the officer. Southgate told him to be careful, but at the same time Betts fired the weapon. The bullet passed between the officer's left arm and his side, grazing the inner part of his arm. As Betts was ready to fire again, the officer made no attempt to apprehend him; however, Betts went into his house and so Southgate went in search of other officers. Within a short time, Police Constables Clark and Holland arrived and they went to Betts' house. Southgate stayed at the front of the house, whilst the other two went around the back. After a short while Southgate entered the house by the street door, and on hearing a whistle from the back of the terrace, he rushed through the front and back room into the garden to find Betts with his back to the garden wall. He was acting very excitedly and had the revolver

Robert Hitchman, Norwich's Chief Constable.

in his hand. He told the officers that he would shoot if they tried to take him into custody. The officers decided to withdraw and returned to the police station, where they made a report.

After hearing the statement from the Chief Constable, the town magistrates granted a warrant for the arrest of Betts. News quickly spread through North Heigham about the events that had occurred, and a large crowd moved towards Northumberland Street in anticipation of the police arresting Betts.

Just before noon, Inspector Guiett, Police Sergeant Hall and Police Constable Airey approached the house, where they were met by Mrs Betts who, with her children, was in despair, not knowing what the outcome of her husband's actions would be. She told them that her husband was in the front bedroom. Hall and Airey started to make their way upstairs, opened the door and ordered Betts to give himself up. Betts fired his gun but missed the officers. He then barricaded the door.

The crowds downstairs, who did not know if the shot had hit one of the policemen, patiently waited for information. A ladder was then obtained by the police and placed by the window, allowing Guiett the chance to speak to Betts. Betts responded by opening up the window and leaning out, and to the shock of all the bystanders he fired his revolver at Guiett, causing a superficial injury to his head. He tied his handkerchief to his head, got into a pony trap that was on the street and was taken back to the police station.

Betts retreated back indoors and next to arrive on the scene was Detective Rushmer and many plain-clothed and uniformed officers. Rushmer went upstairs and spoke with Betts through the closed bedroom door and tried to reason with him, but to no avail. The next hour was taken up with the officers talking with each other whilst the crowd outside were hoping that this violent saga would end peacefully.

At quarter past two that afternoon, two plain-clothes officers arrived at the front door and started to add a ladder to the one already there. Betts came to the window with the revolver still in his hand and pointed it at the crowd, who moved in all directions. He then disappeared back in.

At quarter to three, the Chief Constable, along with Police Constable Mickleburgh, arrived in a Hansom cab. The Chief Constable forced his way through the waiting crowd towards the house; Betts opened up the window and pointed the revolver. Betts was laughing at the situation and acting like a madman. Detective Rushmer once again tried to

Victoria Terrace, where the incident took place.

Northumberland Street today.

get Betts to give himself up. He replied by saying that he would not give himself up in the house, but would do so outside and only in the presence of his solicitor, Mr Sadd. Rushmer agreed to the request and he asked one of the reporters in the crowd to impersonate the solicitor. Rushmer then put the ladder back and just before three o'clock Betts opened the window. After a short chat he descended the ladder and was immediately surrounded by the police constables, who put him in the Hansom cab and took him to the police station, where he was charged with attempting to murder Police Constable Southgate, Inspector Guiett, Police Sergeant Hall and Police Constable Airey. Back at the crime scene, Rushmer entered the bedroom and found the revolver, which was loaded with ball cartridges.

At his trial, Joseph Betts was sentenced to fifteen years in prison and then transferred to Broadmoor Criminal Lunatic Asylum.

Twelve

A LOVERS TRAGEDY

Ellen Baxter was a twenty-four-year-old cook employed by a Mr Read at his house in Rivington, Newmarket Road, and by February 1903 she had been there for six years. Mr Read was also the owner of the St Swithin's Mill, Lower Westwick Street. Ellen had been engaged for some time to James Cooke, aged twenty-nine, who had the nickname of Valentine as he was born on St Valentine's Day. He lived with his widowed mother at Saxmundham, Suffolk, and was employed as a platelayer (maintainer of railway tracks) on the Great Eastern Railway. When he came to visit Ellen he lodged with Mrs Anne Hipper at Melrose Road. The couple were due to be married within a couple of months.

James had served two and a half years with the Field Artillery in India between 1897 and 1898, where he suffered from enteric fever. (Also known as typhoid fever). During the Boer War he fell from his horse and had to undergo three operations, prompting him to suffer from severe mood swings.

On the evening of Wednesday 11 February 1903, James turned up at Rivington without notice to see Ellen at about eight o'clock and the couple went for a walk. At around ten o'clock, whilst the Read family were still having their evening meal and pedestrians were passing the vicinity of the house, four gunshots were fired in quick succession. Mr Read quickly came out of his house to find a group of people looking at the dead bodies of Ellen Baxter and James Cooke lying in pools of blood about 15yds from the road.

The police were immediately called and the bodies were left undisturbed. In a short while Chief Constable Winch and his officers arrived, followed by a police surgeon, Dr Mills. On close inspection, Ellen's body was lying on the left-hand side of the drive, where she had fallen backwards into a flower bed, and her face was half-hidden with a shawl. James was lying under a small lamp on the opposite side of the drive and his hand was doubled up underneath him, holding the revolver. They were 3ft apart. The police quickly took charge of Ellen's bedroom, taking letters and other personal effects. A constable was also stationed outside the Reads' front gateway.

What is left of Rivington House, 101 Newmarket Road, where the tragedy took place. It is now called Norton Court.

The gardens where the tragedy took place.

The inquest took place on 13 February at the Waterman public house, King Street. It was stated that Ellen had a gaping wound in the back of her head and that James had placed the revolver in his mouth and took his own life. It was adjudged that he was guilty of both murder and suicide.

What made this man not only take his own life, but take the life of the woman that he loved so much? Depression plays cruel tricks to the mind, and the horrors that James witnessed during wartime may have driven his decision to commit this terrible crime.

Thirteen

A MURDER, TWO TRIALS AND AN ASYLUM

Christmas 1905, and families in the City of Norwich were enjoying the time together and looking forward to bringing in the New Year. At No. 29 Railway Street, which today no longer exists, lived James Kowen, aged thirty-nine, his wife Rosa, aged thirty-eight, and their two young sons. It was the last house on the left-hand side of the street looking towards the railway.

Theirs was not what could be called a happy marriage. Rosa stayed at home to look after the house and children while James, or Jimmy as he was sometimes known, worked for a cattle loader at the station and received a wage of 26s a week. He was also involved in a partnership with Albert Cooper, owning a pony and trap business which they both did very well out of; James was known to carry up to £20 in a Melford purse.

Rosa liked to have a drink, much to James' displeasure. It was suggested that she drank too much, and was inclined to pawn household items so that she could purchase alcohol. Some said that the couple argued occasionally, whilst others said that they argued daily. What is guaranteed is that their married life was not content. There were also varying reports of the family dog, some found him docile and friendly while others claimed he would bark at the slightest noise. On 28 December an incident would take place that would change their lives forever.

Just after midnight a next-door neighbour heard someone from No. 29 frantically knocking on the wall. Worried that something was wrong, the neighbour left the house to see No. 29 on fire. A messenger was sent to fetch the fire brigade, and whilst this was taking place a group of neighbours rallied together with buckets of water to help diffuse the fire. Fire and smoke were shooting out of the house, and through an upstairs window Rosa Kowen and her two children could be seen. One of the neighbours, Mr Samuel Grand, decided to act and get the woman and children from the house. However, he could

Heigham Street, near to Railway Street, where the Kowen family lived.

not enter via the front door and there were no ladders to hand. He got hold of a plank of wood, which was about the same size as a railway sleeper, and he placed it at an angle to the bedroom window, allowing Rosa and her children to get to safety.

Police Constable Gardiner managed to enter the house and he found the back room in a blaze; it was there that he came across the charred body of James Kowen. As well as the burns, other injuries on the body were found and after a short investigation, Rosa Kowen was arrested. On the following Monday she was put in the dock at Norwich Guildhall on the suspicion of her husband's murder.

The magistrates at the Guildhall that morning were Sir Chas Gilman and Messrs L.E. Willett, W.H. Daking, J. Moore, and H.Z.T. Flowers. Mrs Kowen was described on the charge sheet as Rosa Kowen, thirty-eight years of age and a widow of 29 Railway Street, North Heigham. She was charged with feloniously, wilfully, and with malice aforethought killing and murdering her husband, James Kowen, at Norwich between quarter to eleven at night on 28 December and quarter to one in the morning on 29 December 1905. Mrs Kowen was helped into the dock by a female attendant and she looked around the court nervously as the charges were read out. Mr F.A. Bainbridge from the firm Mills & Reeve appeared on behalf of the police, while Mr W.E. Keefe appeared for Mrs Kowen. Details soon emerged that on the night of the fire James Kowen arrived home and found his wife and two children in bed. Mrs Kowen said, 'My husband took off some of his clothes in the bedroom and then returned downstairs. He said that he wanted to go and read in the back room as there was a nice fire blazing away.'

As Mrs Kowen had only been arrested the day before, Mr Bainbridge asked for an adjournment for a week so that the police could continue with their inquiries. Chief Constable Winch said, 'I saw Mrs Kowen on the Saturday night in the detective department at the police station. I gave the orders for her to be detained and at ten o'clock on the Sunday night I cautioned Mrs Kowen and charged her with wilfully murdering her husband.' Mrs Kowen replied, 'I did not plan to murder him, nor yet to hurt him in anyway.' The magistrates then remanded Mrs Kowen for one week.

The inquest on James Kowen took place at the Waterman public house, King Street, by Mr R.W. Ladell, the city coroner, and Mr F. Smith, was the sworn foreman of the jury. Also present were Mr Bainbridge for the police and Mr Keefe for Mrs Kowen. After an opening speech the jury went to the mortuary to view the body.

Samuel Grand from No. 26 Railway Street said, 'I had known Mr Kowen for about twenty years and that he was a healthy man. He had been at work on the Thursday and that he attended a forester's funeral in the afternoon.' In reply to the foreman, when asked about Kowen's drinking habits, Mr Grand said 'I could not say that James was a teetotaller and that I had never seen him drunk.' The inquest was then adjourned and a certificate of burial was granted.

On a cold and snowy day in January 1906, crowds gathered outside the Shirehall waiting to enter to hear the opening of a murder trial which had gripped Norwich. The case should have been held at the Guildhall, but owing to lack of space it was moved. Many people were turned away from entering due to the fact that the Shirehall was full.

At eleven o'clock Mr Justice Lawrence took his seat and he was accompanied by Mr Carlos Lumsden, the Sheriff of Norwich, and Dr Watson, the Under Sheriff. The prisoner was brought into the dock and informed that she could be seated during the trial. Hushed voices could be heard in the court. As she sat down, she looked at the members of the jury and started to cry.

Mr Horace Avory KC, Mr Haldinstein and Mr Forster Boulton MP, who were instructed by the solicitor Mr W. Lewis on behalf of the Treasury, appeared for the prosecution, and Mr Ernest Wild and Mr Claughton Scott, who were instructed by Mr W.E. Keefe, took charge of the defence.

Mr Avory opened the case and gave a brief history about the deceased and stated that he also made money by grazing cattle on the meadow which adjoined his house as part of an arrangement he had with his father-in-law. He then spoke about the fact that the prisoner drank in secret to hide it from her husband and that most of the arguments between the two were over her drinking. It was claimed that the prisoner was in the habit of sending out for bottles of beer when her husband, whom she referred to as Jimmy, was out of the house. She also kept whiskey in a cupboard, and it was further claimed that before the 28 December she was pawning blankets and linen to purchase alcohol.

Mr Avory also revealed that she had told Mrs Hasted, who was employed to pawn the items, that she did not like the way that her husband was treating her and that she wanted to go to live in London, leaving the children with her husband. Avory stated that there was no doubt that the deceased was violent towards his wife, as on more than one occasion she called the attention of the neighbours to see black eyes and bruises which she said had been caused by her husband after he had accused her of being drunk. She was also reported to have said to a neighbour, 'I should like to see him brought in stiff. I would have a good drink over it.' She was a woman who displayed violent language and was physically strong; she told Mrs Hasted that during a quarrel with her husband, she had taken up one of the chains in the room and thrown it at him, hitting the door instead which had cracked from top to bottom. On another occasion when a quarrel took place in front of Albert Cooper, the prisoner said 'I will be hung for you.' Mr Avory then went on to say that the real question in the case would be was the murder committed by the prisoner, or was it that another person could have come into that room and committed the crime?

Ethel Tills, who lived with her parents next door to the Kowens, said:

On about midnight on 28 December I heard the prisoner knocking on her bedroom from my own bedroom and shouting out 'Ethel, Ethel, I believe my house is on fire.' I then called on my father and we both went to find a policeman. When we got back I noticed that the prisoner had her blouse on back to front. During the rest of the evening and in the morning the prisoner said nothing to me about her husband, and it was only in the afternoon that she said 'Ethel, is this not dreadful, I wish I had stayed up for him, and then this would not have happened.'

The wife of Samuel Grand was next to give evidence, and said:

Whilst the prisoner was throwing items of clothing and a cash box out of the windows, someone shouted out 'Where's Jimmy?' and the prisoner replied 'I heard him go out the back. I don't know whether he has gone on the meadow.' The prisoner was very cool and collected. When the body was being bought out from the house the prisoner was standing by Miss Tills' house and asked who the body was. I replied that it was a neighbour nicknamed Yankee; the prisoner became excited, and clasped her hands and said 'No, it is my husband. Yankee would not be in my house at this time of night.'

In the past I seen bruises on the prisoner's arms and was told that the deceased had caused this when the prisoner had taken too much time to take off one of her children's boots. I was told by the prisoner, 'I would like to see him brought in stiff.' I said that she should leave her husband and that if she went to the police court she would have to tell them all about their business which would not be of help to either. Once late at night Mrs Kowen was seen by me throwing stones at the bedroom window. The Kowen's son, Clifford, called out for his mother to stop and the deceased was heard to shout out 'I won't have the drunken in anymore.'

Mrs Tills, Ethel's mother, then gave evidence and said:

I was on friendly terms with the prisoner and I had seen her bruises and believed that she would leave her husband over his temper. On the night in question I heard the prisoner call out from the bedroom 'Murder!' My son delivered to the prisoner a pint of best ale at least twice a week but I could not recall seeing her worse for drink. A week before the tragedy Mr

The Waterman public house, King Street, where the inquest of James Kowen took place.

The Shirehall, where the trials of Rosa Kowen took place.

Kowen had accused Mrs Kowen of being drunk. When the body was bought out of the house I told Mrs Kowen that I believed the body was that of her husband and she replied 'Never, never. What shall I do? Oh, if I had stayed up for him this would not have happened.' She also said, 'He has hurt me a good many times, but I have never hurt him.' It was untrue that Mrs Kowen was in the habit of drinking in my house with me.

Other evidence was given by twelve-year-old neighbour Sarah Webster, who said, 'I purchased two pints of paraffin for Mrs Kowen on the Wednesday during the Christmas week.'

A solicitor's clerk and friend of the Kowens, William Alfred Hindle said:

I had tea with them on the evening of the tragedy. There had only been slight quarrels between husband and wife and to my knowledge there had never been anything in the nature of violence or threats. Mrs Kowen had not been drinking on the evening of the tragedy and that Mr Kowen had a Melford purse in his inside coat pocket as a rule, and his loose money in his trouser pocket.

Mr Kowen's business partner, Albert Cooper, was next to give evidence and said:

For our business dealings, I had paid Mr Kowen £14 10s between last October and Christmas. Mrs Kowen had complained to me that her husband kept her short of money, although Mr Kowen gave her a sovereign each week. I had seen a bruise on her arm. A year previous, Mrs Kowen had said in my presence that she would hang for her husband and I took it as a joke.

Mr Wild, acting for the defence, then said, 'It has been suggested that the dog would not let anyone pass him.' Mr Cooper replied 'That was not the case.' Asked about the time Mrs Kowen said that she would hang for her husband, he said 'It arose over dinner and that the deceased also took it to be a joke.'

On the second day of the trial, George Edwards, also known as Yankee, said:

I had been in the employ of Mr Kowen for at least five years, and on the afternoon of the tragedy I had used the chopper and the axe and then replaced them in the shed. I did not see any blood on the items, but I could not say if there had been and I do not know whether I cut my finger or not. The paraffin can was usually kept under the sink in the wash house and I can confirm that I fetched two pints of oil for Mrs Kowen on Christmas day. I had slept in one of the sheds for five or six weeks and had never seen any strangers about. I went to bed at eleven o'clock and got up at five o'clock. On the evening of the tragedy at about half past seven Mr Kowen kissed his wife and boy and went out. The last time that I saw him alive was at half past eight at his office at the cattle pens. At twenty past eleven I was with a man called Richardson at Railway Road and I then went to the shed.

When asked about the dog, he said:

It would lie down when anyone told it to do so. Several people used the gate that led onto the meadows. I heard nothing during the night and only found out what had happened in the morning. The couple got on fairly well and had words occasionally. I had seen Mrs Kowen with a black eye and bruises, but it had been two years previous and that the gate to the meadows was always unlocked and in constant use.

The next witness was Mrs Maria Hasted, who said:

I have known the couple for thirteen years and I sometimes did work for them. The couple often quarrelled, and sometimes these had been violent, but not in my presence. Once Mrs Kowen had a black eye and that her husband caused it because she was drunk. I had seen Mrs Kowen worse for drink and that she sent children to get drink for her and that she went to Mrs Tills' house to drink. A row took place when Mrs Kowen wanted to employ a charwoman and Mrs Kowen said to me that 'Jimmy was coming for her, and she took up a chair and flung it at him.' On another occasion Mrs Kowen expressed a wish that her husband was in the asylum, adding she would have 'a rare old drunk.'

Mrs Hasted caused a sensation in court when she talked about the Kowens' younger son's nosebleed. She said:

Reginald came into the house and began to talk and his mother told him to be quiet, and then taking up a cane, she drew it across the boy's face, causing his nose to bleed. I had pawned a watch, blankets and sheets for Mrs Kowen for 19s and that Mrs Kowen needed the money to pay some bills, but later said that the money was for her to leave her husband to live in London. On the Saturday after the tragedy, I met Mrs Kowen at Mrs Tills' house where Mrs Kowen said to me 'Good God, Maria, have the tecs [police] been to see you?' I replied 'No' and she then asked for the items to be redeemed from the pawnbrokers as they may be wanted.

Mr Wild then asked questions about Mrs Kowen's alleged drinking habits and she said, 'I had taken back up to eight bottles so that Mr Kowen would not see them.' Asked if she did not like Mrs Kowen, Mrs Hasted said, 'Well I am accustomed to pawn things, but I don't pawn things for drink. I have to keep my children.'

Next to give evidence was Mr E.F. Winch, the Chief Constable of Norwich. He said, 'I arrived at the house just after one o'clock in the morning. The body of the deceased was lying in the yard. I entered the living room where the fire had been put out.'

He then produced pieces of wallpaper from the living room which were splashed with blood. He also revealed a piece of the flooring under the hearthrug in the living room and the hearthrug itself, pointing out paraffin stains on both. The axe and the chopper were then produced, along with a brick from the cellar wall which had a clot of blood on it. He then said, 'The position of the blood was consistent with someone having placed a hand against the wall in order to stoop down.'

Mrs Kowen's blouse that she was wearing on the evening was shown and the Winch said:

Against a white background red spots could be seen. I then went to Mrs Tills' house where Mrs Kowen said that she took her son to bed as he had a nosebleed and she later took some water upstairs to wash his nose and face and then washed her hands in the same water. Mrs Kowen then told me that she went to bed and was woken up by a noise. She smelt smoke and heard the breaking of glass. She went downstairs but had difficulty in entering the room because of the smoke. She went to the window and shouted out 'Fire!' She then dressed her sons and took off her dirty nightdress and put on a bodice, petticoat, and skirt. She said that her husband had complained of pains, and she had advised him to go to see a doctor. She thought that her husband might have taken ill and fallen into the fire. She said that she used a hammer which was on the mantelpiece to break coal for the fire. Half a sovereign was found on the mantelpiece which Mrs Kowen said was for the housekeeping. When Mrs Kowen was arrested on the Saturday night and charged, she said, 'I never murdered him. I am not guilty.' On the Sunday she said, 'I did not plan to murder him nor yet hurt him in any way.'

The Chief Constable admitted to Mr Wild that a part of his evidence was theory, and said 'There were two distinct pools of blood and Mrs Kowen told me quite voluntarily. There was blood and water on the clothing that made up the bonfire and the only article of clothing with blood on it was the blouse.'

Next to give evidence was Detective Inspector High who worked alongside the Chief Constable. He said 'The Melford purse has not been found and a handkerchief found in the pocket of Mr Kowen's clothing was covered in blood and I found two labelled bottles that smelt of whiskey.'

Dr R.J. Mills, a police surgeon, said:

I examined the body of Mr Kowen, and the left side, head and face were badly burnt. On the head were twenty-six wounds of which some were incised and contused wounds. On the top of the head was a wound which went through the skull bone, sharply bevelling off a piece of the skull, and lifting it up from the brain. There were eight incised wounds which were caused by a straight-bladed instrument. All the wounds could have been caused by a chopper, with one being caused by an axe. There were six wounds on the right side of the head which could have been caused with the head of a hammer. In the centre of the forehead was a compressed fracture of the skull bone which was driven into the brain. All of the upper teeth were knocked out, two out of their sockets, and the others broken off. A contusion on the chest was caused by considerable violence. If Mr Kowen had received these blows whilst sitting down on a chair some of the spots of blood, but not all, would be produced. The handle of the hammer had been washed and I found blood on one side of the chopper. The bowl with soapy water was given to me, but no blood was found in it. The spots of blood on Mrs Kowen's blouse might have come from her son's nosebleed.

Cross-examined by Mr Wild, Dr Mills said 'The contusion on the neck could have been caused by throttling. This and the contusion on the chest were caused before Mr Kowen died.'

Whilst hearing this evidence many ladies in the court felt faint and left the building, while Mrs Kowen burst into tears.

Dr Pepper, a medical advisor to the Home Office, said:

> There is the possibility that the axe caused the wounds that penetrated the skull, but it was extremely improbable. I have been to the house and seen the room and that it would have been difficult to wield an axe like that in the room. The edge of the axe was far too broad to have cracked the skull.

Mr Horace Avory addressed the Jury and said:

> There has been undisputable evidence that whoever committed this murder, deliberately made the fire for the purpose of destroying evidence of the crime. It was improbable that the assailant hit the deceased on the front of the head and would have turned him over in order to inflict the wounds on the back of the head. It was more probable that the wounds were inflicted in rapid succession from the back. It was impossible for any intruder to have entered the house and committed the murder without the prisoner, who slept in the room above, being disturbed. Whatever the motive from which she acted, it must have been her hand which inflicted the injuries and caused the fire.

On the third day of the trial, Albert Cooper was recalled at the request of the jury. One of the questions asked was if Mr Kowen was sober on the night of the tragedy and another was whether it was customary for the dog to be unchained. Mr Cooper could not say. George Edwards was then recalled and he said that the dog was let loose at night and that a few weeks previously the dog's collar had been lost or stolen.

In his summing up for the defence, Mr Ernest Wild said:

> I do not know that I have ever met a case of murder in which there is so little dispute as to the salient facts. It was said by the Crown that the woman must have done it. Naturally, before they dared bring a charge of this terrible gravity, they had hunted about, quite legitimately, for some antecedent facts that could fairly point to a motive for the perpetration of a deed of such ghastly horror, and all the life of these people had been investigated, a sort of book of remembrance had been opened against the prisoner, and everything that she said, every idle word that she had used, had been brought forward in court.

Mr Wild spoke in length about the alleged unhappy life of the couple. He then spoke about the witnesses and the comment that Mrs Kowen was supposed to have said about wanting her husband dead and her alleged drinking. He continued by saying:

> Whoever did this murder must have got a lot of blood upon him or her. There were twenty-six wounds, and some had been inflicted only by the use of terrible force. Then there was the throttling, in which great pressure must have been brought to bear upon the deceased's chest.

He then pointed to Mrs Kowen in the dock and said 'Was that the arm that wielded those terrible weapons, or whose strength that pressed on the chest and afterwards moved the body?' He went on to say:

It was unlikely that she would have the strength, even if she had the courage to do it. What evidence has been produced to show any signs of blood, fire or paraffin on the stairs or upstairs? If she did this thing, she must have been covered with blood, whilst in setting fire to the bonfire afterwards she must have been spattered with paraffin. Yet she is supposed to have gone upstairs afterwards, but there were no traces of either blood or anything else on the handle of the stairs door, or the stairs themselves, or in the room above. Then there is the dog and there was a time when it dominated the case. The prosecution said how could an assassin who left the house pass such a yard dog? It was a regular Cerberus keeping the gates of the yard. It has now been proved to be a pacifist dog, and therefore out goes the dog. There were two opportunities for a man to get in from outside. One was when Mr Kowen was upstairs taking off his collar and the other when he was in the water closet. Whoever did this did not desire to be thought to be the murderer. He wanted it to be looked upon as an accident, and therefore whoever did it knew something of the ways of the place and having killed Mr Kowen, stopped, took the things to his hand, the children's clothes, etc, and made a fire and used the paraffin.

The prosecution said that a sufficient noise must have been made to awaken Mrs Kowen. There probably was not much noise. If there was much noise it would have been heard by Mrs Tills or Mr Geary. There was also the evidence of the Melford purse which had as much as £20 in it on 17 December. But where is the Melford purse? The prosecution said it was burnt in the fire, but whenever the prosecution get into a difficulty, they burn things in the fire. The back door was unlocked, as was the door leading from the scullery into the living room, and the door leading from the living room into the parlour, which was perhaps the most important door. Therefore, the murderer, who must have been a man, could come in through the doors, probably left open by the deceased when he went to the water closet. A customer, knowing of Mr Kowen's habits, followed him, not around the passage by No. 29, but down by No. 25, and turned around at the back. Having waited behind the parlour door until the deceased came in, the assailant came at him from behind, felling him without noise. The man dropped down, throttling took place, preventing the deceased from crying out. There was a short struggle. Then the man thrust his hands into the blood stained pockets and took away the Melford purse. The man then made the bonfire, used the paraffin, set fire to it and escaped with the weapon used. Whoever did this murder must have been covered in blood and the only item produced by the prosecution was the blouse worn by Mrs Kowen which had a few spots of blood on it which was more likely caused by her son's nosebleed.

Mr Wild ended his closing speech at half past twelve, having spoken for two-and-a-half hours. In his own summing up, the judge said, 'There are many facts beyond dispute. No evidence has been called by the other side. The question was did these facts establish the guilt of the prisoner? Your attention has been called to the fact that there is no direct evidence and the case rested on circumstantial evidence.'

The jury went out to deliberate and were out for two hours and twenty-five minutes but could not agree on a verdict. They were then discharged and Mrs Kowen was further remanded until the next Assizes.

The grave of James Kowen, who is buried at Earlham Cemetery.

The second trial took place on 16 June before Mr Justice A.T. Lawrence. Ernest Wild again acted for Mrs Kowen, but the defence was led by Mr F.K. North who objected to five members of the jury and had them replaced. Mr Wild spoke for two-and-a-quarter hours for the closing speech, and once again the jury failed to agree upon a verdict. Mrs Kowen was further remanded in prison to await her fate.

Meanwhile, the Norwich Watch Committee elevated Detective Inspector High, Detective Superintendent Goldsmith and Police Constable Gardiner to higher grades of pay. Chief Constable Winch received £5 for his out-of-pocket expenses and a further £5 to be distributed to other officers at his discretion.

On Thursday 5 July, a telegram was received by Major Fowler, the Governor of Norwich Prison, from the Attorney General in regards to the case against Mrs Kowen. *Nolle prosequi* had been entered, meaning that Mrs Kowen would not face further prosecution and would be released. At around three o'clock in the afternoon, a cab arrived at the prison

Norwich Station, where Rosa Kowen took a train to London after she was released from Norwich Prison.

with Mrs Kowen's father and her solicitor, Mr W.E. Keefe. A few members of the press were waiting after being tipped off that Mrs Kowen was being released. The cab then sped away from the prison towards Thorpe Station, where she took a train to London to a secret destination. It would have been extremely difficult for Mrs Kowen to have gone back to her marital home, or to have even stayed in Norwich.

Within two weeks the contents of the Kowens' house was auctioned, with many people turning up through morbid curiosity. Among the many people there was George 'Yankee' Edwards, who was now looking after the Kowens' dog. After an incident in London involving Rosa Kowen, she was committed to the London County Council Asylum and certified as insane. She was then taken to an asylum in Kent, and later transferred to the Hellesdon Hospital in Norwich where she remained until her death on 4 February 1927. Some would say that it was a fitting finish for a woman who had gone through two murder trials only to be released, while there were those who believed that Rosa Kowen was just another victim. Both Rosa and James are buried at Earlham Cemetery.

Fourteen

THE SLAYING OF ELEANOR HOWARD

The parish of Old Catton lies about three miles to the north of Norwich. It now sits on the eastern edge of Norwich International Airport. In 1987 Old Catton was twinned with Lavaré, which is about twenty miles east of Le Mans in the Sarthe District in south-west France.

Eleanor Elizabeth Howard, also known as Nellie, was nineteen years of age and lived with her grandparents at Radford Hall, where they were in service. Nellie's boyfriend, nineteen-year-old Horace Larter, lived with his parents at Ber Street Gates. He worked for his father as a fish dealer and kept a fish stall outside the Agriculture Hall at Bank Plain. They had been seeing each other for two years, but in recent times Nellie had been seeing less of Horace. On Thursday 29 October 1908, Horace brutally killed Nellie, the woman he loved.

The inquest took place on the following Monday at the Maid's Head Inn, headed by the county coroner, Mr H.R. Culley, and a jury. The prisoner was brought from Norwich Prison in a cab by two warders, who remained at his side throughout the hearing. His right hand was in bandages. He showed no emotion until a statement that he made in his cell was read out, in which he said goodbye to his sister after telling her that he had killed Nellie. The jury then viewed the body which was held at the coach-house of the inn.

The first witness was Nellie's grandfather, William Howard, a farm steward of Haynford, who said:

My granddaughter had lived with me for the past few months. She was acquainted with Horace Larter, with whom she had been friendly for some time. She had arranged to meet him last Thursday at Norwich, and left Haynford about two o'clock, and I expected her home about seven o'clock in the evening, but I did not see her again alive. About three months ago I

Agriculture Hall, Norwich, where Horace Larter worked on a fish stall.

The Maids Head Inn, Old Catton, where the inquest into the murder of Eleanor 'Nellie' Howard took place.

heard her say that Larter had threatened to shoot her if he found her with anyone else. To my knowledge, she had not walked out with anyone else. She was a steady going, respectable girl. I remember that she received a letter on Thursday morning.

Police Sergeant Slater handed the letter to the coroner, who read parts of it out:

So if we are to part we can part the very best of friends. So do come up, and we can go to the exhibition together. Hope to meet you at two o'clock, as I shall come to meet you, so do come up if for the last time. Glad you like my chocolates. So do come up to Norwich for the sake of the time we have had. Hope you have time to write. My mother would like to see you Thursday, as father's out, and give my affectionate love to you. I remain yours, Horace. I shall come if you have not time to write, so I meet you coming along. Start at two.

George Howard, a cabman from Norwich said:

I am acquainted with the deceased and with Larter. I saw the latter on Thursday morning, when he said he was going to have a day off to see his sweetheart. About half past five in the afternoon he and the deceased came to see me on the cab rank. Larter asked me to drive them home to his father's house. On the way there we stopped at the Norwich Arms. Here we had a drink. The deceased did not get out of the cab; Larter took her a glass of port wine. We stopped there about six minutes and then proceeded to the Gate House, which both the deceased and Larter entered. They were there about a few minutes, after which they took the cab back to the rank, where Larter asked me to drive them to Catton, Maid's Head. I said I could not as I was ordered that evening, and they then left in the direction of Magdalen Street. The time was about six o'clock.

A tram-car conductor named Chaplin said, 'On Thursday evening, the deceased and Larter boarded my car at the General Post Office and left at the Whalebone Inn, Catton, at six o'clock. They went up St Clement's Hill, and I noticed that they called at a sweetshop. I noticed that Larter had been drinking.'

Police Sergeant Slater was then called to testify:

On Thursday night I was on the road leading from Old Catton to the Lone Barn, Spixworth, when at about ten minutes to nine o'clock, I saw a figure lying on the right-hand side of the road, about a quarter of a mile on the Norwich side of the Lone Barn. It was a very dark night, and, turning on my lamp I found the figure was the body of the deceased, who was lying on her left side, her head resting on her left arm. She was covered with blood, which had flowed from a wound in her neck and another in her face. The body was getting cold. The deceased was fully dressed. Her hat had not been removed. The white cotton glove she was wearing was saturated with blood.

I went for assistance to the Lone Barn and despatched a man named Laws for Dr Flack, of Norwich, and Inspector Roy, of the County Police. Dr Flack on arrival made a superficial examination of the body as it lay on the ground assisted by my bull's eye and a cab lamp; it was then removed on a cart to the Maid's Head Inn. On searching the body I found in the dress

Spixworth Road, Old Catton, where the body of Eleanor 'Nellie' Howard was found.

pocket a purse, 1*s*, 2*d*, a key, and a packet of chocolate. Next morning, as soon as it was light, I went to the spot where I made the horrible discovery, and searched it thoroughly, finding spots of blood on the road for 150yds in the direction of Haynford. I was then accompanied by Inspector Roy, and going in the direction of Norwich we found another spot of blood on the roadway a quarter of a mile from where the body had lain. At the Maid's Head we found five or six spots of blood on the bar floor, and from what the landlady, Mrs Cullum, told us, we suspected Larter. We proceeded to Norwich and found him in custody.

Mrs Cullum said:

I saw Larter on Thursday night between a quarter past seven and a quarter to eight. He did not remain more than ten minutes. He called for half a pint of ale, which was served to him. He drank it, with the exception of what he spilled on the floor. He appeared to be in a very excited state, and used very bad language. There was blood on his right hand and mud on his coat, which he explained was the result of a fall from a bicycle. He asked for a second drink, which I refused to serve, telling him to clear off. He left the house a minute or so afterwards. When I closed the door after he left, I noticed bloodstains on the bar floor.

Mrs Florence Ludkin was then called, and she was very distressed as she gave evidence:

I knew the deceased, and Larter is my brother. On Thursday night, about half past seven my brother came to my house and he said, 'I'm a bit boozy. Can I come in?' He asked me where my husband was, and I told him that he was in bed. My brother sat down and asked me if I had a cup of tea for him. I told him that I had not. He then said. 'I have cut my little finger. Can I wash it?' I replied, 'No, you will mess the place up, let me do it for you.' I also told him to sit still on the chair or he would fall over, but he got up and walked to the door. He said to me, 'Will you shake hands with me for the last time? I have killed Nellie.' He then walked away from the door, and when outside the house he said to me, 'I shall give myself up to the first constable I come to.'

Horace Larter then shouted out, 'Goodbye Florrie!' In a frail and emotional voice, the young woman called out, 'Goodbye Horrie!'

Henry William Wright, landlord of the Whalebone, said:

I spoke to Larter after he visited the house on Thursday afternoon on two occasions, first between half past two and three o'clock and on the second between three o'clock and half past. On the last occasion he was accompanied by the deceased, and they came from the direction of Old Catton. The young woman had a lemonade and Larter a whisky and soda. They stayed about five minutes and left together in the direction of the city. I next saw Larter in the evening, between half past seven and half past eight. He was alone. He called for a small lemonade. He was rather excited. There was blood on his hands and clothing, and I mentioned this to him. Larter replied that he had met with a cycle accident just before. I noticed that he had an open clasp knife in his waistcoat pocket. It was open, the blade protruding through the bottom of the waistcoat. I ventured to suggest that it was owing to him having the open knife in his pocket that he had sustained the cuts on his hand in falling of the bicycle, but Larter made no reply. I advised him to close the knife and put it in his pocket, and he did so.

A tram-car conductor named William Knivett said, 'I spoke with Larter in my car from Magdalen Street to Catton between four and five o'clock on Thursday afternoon.'

William Arnold, a farm assistant at Buxton Lammas, stated:

I picked up the umbrella and walking stick, I was with others cycling home from Norwich on Thursday night about a quarter past ten. The umbrella was lying by the side of the road and the stick on the grass by the roadside, about 2yds away from it, at a spot about a quarter of a mile from where the body was found.

Mabel Hilda Smithson, Nellie's cousin who lived with her at Haynford, identified the umbrella as the same one that the deceased took with her when she left home on Thursday afternoon to go to meet Larter.

Inspector Ebbage, of the Norwich City Police, then gave a brief account about the surrender of Larter at Norwich Guildhall on Friday morning.

Police Constable Poulter, who was placed in charge of Larter in a cell at the County Police station, said:

The prisoner made the following statement to me voluntarily. 'I met her at about three o'clock on Elm Hill. I had rather a job to get her to come with me, because I could see she didn't want me. I took her for a cab drive round Norwich, and went to the Norwich Arms in Ber Street. I treated her to two glasses of port, and I also treated the cabman. I gave a man 3d to hold the horse while the cabman came inside with me. She would not come in the pub herself. I quite intended enjoying myself as I knew she did not want me, and I had made up my mind to kill her. I went down to Pearsons the same morning and a bought a clasp knife, which I gave a shilling for. I felt as if I could have murdered anyone if I saw them speaking to her. I loved her so, and this is all through love and jealousy. This is what hate and love will do. I intended her not to make a fool of me.

After we had enjoyed ourselves in Norwich, I walked along the road to take her home. It was about six o'clock when we started quarrelling. She told me she did not want me, and I said, 'You sha'nt have anyone else.' That was about half past six, when I felt like a madman. I caught her by the throat with one hand, and stabbed her twice with the other. Just as she was turning round when I thought to walk away, I stabbed her again, when she fell down and never spoke again. I stood by her quite five minutes, and I thought I would do myself in. Then a change came over me. I knelt down in a pool of blood, which you will see on my trousers, and kissed her when she was dead. And then I pinned a buttonhole on her and left. Never mind, I suppose her soul is now in Heaven. If it were not for her people this never would have happened. They have been saying things about me so I should not have her, and I think it is about the best thing I could have done. I have had this on my mind a long time.

Dr Flack, of Magdalen Road, said:

I examined the body as it lay when discovered on the roadside by Police Sergeant Slater. On the left cheek was a wound 1½in in length, and also a punctured one on the neck on the right side over the collar bone. The latter wound would admit my finger to a distance of over 2in. A post-mortem showed a third wound in the back, which just missed the spinal column. The collarbone wound was in the shape of a wide V, each side of the V being a ½in in length. That was the fatal wound, as it severed a main artery leading to the arm, and deceased could not have lived more than two minutes after its infliction.

The coroner then asked Larter if he wished to make any addition to the statements he had given, and in a clear voice he replied, 'No, sir.'

The inquest had lasted six and a half hours, and the jury, without leaving the room, returned a verdict of wilful murder against Larter, who turned to the jury and said, 'Thank you gentlemen, one and all.'

At the Shirehall on Saturday 7 November 1908, a large crowd awaited outside hoping to gain entrance to listen to the magistrates' hearing. Inside, the building was packed. When the charge was read out, Larter nodded his head and took his seat between two prison warders. Inspector Ebbage of the City Police gave his evidence of when Larter first confessed to the crime. Larter rose from his seat and said, 'If I had made a good job of it, as I told the police officer I intended, I should not be here now.' He was then committed to trial at the Assizes.

At the trial, on 27 January 1909, Mr H.H. Lawless and Mr G.H.B. Kenrick were instructed to prosecute on behalf of the Treasury, and Mr A.L. Taylor, at the request of the judge, was present to defend the prisoner. On being arraigned by the clerk, the prisoner replied in a loud voice, 'Guilty, my Lord.'

The judge wished to clarify this plea, 'You say you are guilty?'

Larter replied, 'Yes, my Lord.'

'Do you know what it is you are pleading guilty to?'

'Yes, my Lord.'

'Do you know the consequences?'

'Yes my Lord.'

The judge went on, 'There is a learned counsel who has been kind enough to say he will defend you. Under these circumstances, do you still wish to plead guilty? I don't, however, wish to interfere if you know what you are doing. That is all.'

The prisoner then said, 'I beg your pardon, my Lord.' The judge repeated himself and the prisoner replied, 'I would sooner plead guilty, my Lord.'

The judge made one final enquiry, 'Do you understand, thoroughly understand, what you are doing, and what the consequences are?'

'Yes, my Lord.'

The judge then simply said, 'Very well.'

The Clerk of the Assizes then asked the prisoner if he had anything to say why judgement of death should not be pronounced upon you according to law? The prisoner replied, 'No, my Lord.'

The judge then put on his black cap and he spoke:

Horace Larter, you have pleaded guilty to a charge of wilful murder, and you have done so after having been reminded by me as to what the consequences to you must necessarily be. Upon the facts of the case there can be no doubt whatever of your crime – a cruel crime, upon a girl with whom you had been on friendly terms, and who if I may judge from the letters which had passed between you, had been, at all events, an affectionate girl to you. For some small reason, some slight, hardly amounting to a quarrel, as far as I can make out, between her relations and you, you make up your mind to take that girl's life.

The act was a premeditated act – of that there can be no doubt. You furnished yourself with the weapon – a knife – with which the murder was accomplished. You invited the girl to meet you in Norwich, and after spending the afternoon, up to about six o'clock, you walk with her towards her home, and on the way you stab her in the neck and cause her death. Nothing more cruel, more hard hearted, can possibly be. It only remains for me to pass upon you the sentence which the law inflicts upon those who are guilty of this offence, and that is that you be taken from this place to a lawful prison and thence to the place of execution, and that you there be hanged by the neck until you are dead, and that your body be buried within the precincts of the prison in which you shall have been confined before your execution. May the Lord have mercy on your soul.

Norwich solicitors Mills & Reeve presented a petition for reprieve to the Home Secretary, and on 9 February 1909 the firm received a reply which said that after a medical enquiry into the mental condition of the prisoner, the Home Secretary has advised His Majesty to respite the capital sentence with a view to the immediate removal of Larter to the Broadmoor Criminal Lunatic Asylum.

With a short spell at Rampton Branch from 1912 to 1916, Horace Larter spent the rest of his life at Broadmoor and died there in 1941.

Fifteen

HANGMEN WHO CAME TO NORWICH

Most hangmen had a separate profession whilst acting as an executioner. These are a few examples:

William Calcraft

William Calcraft (1800-1879) was from Little Baddow, near Chelmsford, in Essex. He was the longest serving executioner of all, working from 1829-1874, and was noted for his 'short drops', causing most of his victims to strangle to death. It is not known precisely how many executions he carried out, but it is estimated at somewhere between 400 and 450, including those of at least thirty-five women.

He claimed to have invented the leather waist belt with wrist straps for pinioning the prisoner's arms. One of the nooses he used is still on display at Lancaster Castle; it is a very short piece of ¾in rope with a loop worked into one end, with the free end of the rope passed through it and terminating in a hook. This was then attached to the chain fixed to the gallows beam.

William Marwood

William Marwood (1820-1883) was from Horncastle, Lincolnshire, and was an exectutioner between 1874 and 1883. Marwood was a cobbler by trade who had, over the years, taken a great interest in the art of hanging and felt that it could be improved. He had never hanged anyone or even assisted at an execution, but at the age of fifty-four persuaded the authorities at Lincoln Prison to let him carry out the hanging of William Frederick Horry on the 1 April 1872. The execution went off without a hitch and impressed the governor of the prison as Marwood introduced the 'long drop' method of hanging. He realised that if the prisoner was to be given a drop of 6-10ft depending upon his weight and with the noose correctly positioned, death would be nearly instantaneous due to the neck being broken. The long drop removed all the gruesome struggling and convulsing from the proceedings and was, undoubtedly, far less cruel to the prisoner and far less trying to the governor and staff of the prison who, since the abolition of public hangings, had to witness the spectacle at close quarters.

There was a famous rhyme about Marwood at the time which went, 'If Pa killed Ma, who'd kill Pa? Marwood.' Marwood was something of a celebrity and had business cards printed which said 'William Marwood Public Executioner, Horncastle, Lincolnshire' and had the words 'Marwood Crown Office' over the door of his shop. In his eleven years of service, he hanged 181 people, including nine women, before dying of inflammation of the lungs on 4 September 1883.

James Berry

James Berry (1852-1913) of Heckmondwike, Yorkshire, carried out 130 hangings between 1884-1891, including those of five women. He was the first British executioner to write his memoirs, *My Experiences as an Executioner.* He was, like Marwood, proud of his calling and both had their own waxworks in Madame Tussauds. Berry had previously been a policeman in Bradford and had met Marwood and became acquainted with his methods. One notable and unfortunate experience took place at one of his executions at Norwich Castle on the 30 November 1885. The condemned man, Robert Goodale, weighed fifteen stone and was in poor physical condition, and was horrifically decapitated by the force of the drop. Fortunately, this appears to have been an isolated incident.

James Billington

James Billington (1847-1901) was from Farnworth, near Bolton, in Lancashire. He served as a hangman between 1884 and 1901. Billington had a lifelong fascination with hanging and had unsuccessfully applied for Marwood's post before managing to secure the hangman's position for the county of Yorkshire. He later succeeded James Berry as the executioner for London and the Home Counties in 1892.

Henry Albert Pierrepoint

Henry Pierrepoint (1874-1922) was from Bradford, Yorkshire, and assisted at thirty hangings and carried out seventy-five executions himself between 1901 and 1910. He took great pride in his work and calculated the drops most carefully. He is said to never have bungled a single hanging.

Albert Pierrepoint

Albert Pierrepoint (1905-1992) of Clayton, near Bradford in Yorkshire, was by far the most prolific hangman of the twentieth century. The son of Henry Albert Pierrepoint, he was an assistant or principal at the hangings of an estimated 434 people, including sixteen women, in his twenty-four years of service in this country and abroad between 1932 and 1956. His tally of executions was greatly increased as a result of the Second World War, working in various countries, such as the United Kingdom, Germany, Egypt, Gibraltar and Austria. Albert was to execute fourteen men convicted of espionage and treason during and immediately after the Second World War. In England and Wales, Albert assisted at twenty-nine hangings and carried out 138 civilian executions for murder as principal, including those of the last four women to be sentenced to hang.

Right: A newspaper article on the lectures of James Berry.

Below: Tools of the trade. An execution box was sent to county prisons from HMP Pentonville.

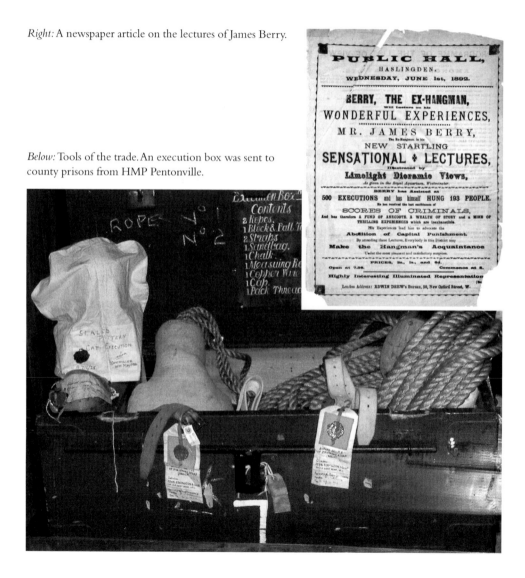

LIST OF SOURCES

Capital Punishment UK (www.capitalpunishmentuk.org)
Celebrated Trials of all Countries, 1836 (Edited by John Jay Smith)
Executed Today (www.executedtoday.com)
Norfolk Online Access to Heritage (www.noah.norfolk.gov.uk)
The Eastern Daily Press (including the *Norfolk Chronicle*, where the trials were reported)
The Jewish Museum, London (www.jewishmuseum.org.uk)
The National Archives (www.nationalarchives.gov.uk)
Recollections of John Thurtell by Pierce Egan
Wikipedia (www.wikipedia.org)

Other titles published by The History Press

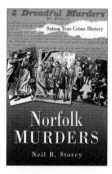

Norfolk Murders
NEIL R. STOREY

Contained within the pages of this book are the stories behind some of the most notorious murders in Norfolk's history. Using contemporary illustrations and tracing the stories through the words of those who were actually there on the ground, he re-creates the drama of case and courtroom. *Norfolk Murders* is a unique re-examination of the darker side of the county's past.

978 0 7509 4366 6

Murder & Crime Boston
DOUGLAS WYNN

The town of Boston lies alongside the peaceful River Witham and has the appearance of a tranquil place where nothing much has ever happened. This first impression is misleading. In terms of murder and mayhem, Boston has a tale to rival anywhere else in Lincolnshire. These fourteen tales of true murder from the late nineteenth and early twentieth centuries, compiled by renowned local author Douglas Wynn, will fascinate anyone wanting to know more about Boston's dark history.

978 0 7524 5544 0

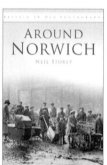

Around Norwich
NEIL R. STOREY

Around Norwich is not just another book on this fine city. Combining many previously unpublished photographs of outstanding quality and interest with well-researched captions, including many new facts and stories, one of the county's foremost local historians has created a fascinating narrative of the city, suburbs, people, shops and events of the past. This book will be an enduring and nostalgic record, of interest to anyone who knows and loves the City of Norwich.

978 0 7524 5378 1

Haunted Norwich
DAVID CHISNELL

From heartstopping accounts of apparitions, manifestations and related supernatural phenomena *Haunted Norwich* contains new and well-known spooky stories from around the city. This fascinating collection of strange sightings and happenings in the city's streets, churches, public houses and historic buildings is sure to appeal to anyone wanting to know more about the haunted heritage of Norwich.

978 0 7524 3700 2

Visit our website and discover thousands of other History Press books.

www.thehistorypress.co.uk